STILL LIFE

THE OBJECT IN AMERICAN ART, 1915–1995

SELECTIONS FROM THE METROPOLITAN MUSEUM OF ART

Lowery Stokes Sims and Sabine Rewald

With a contribution by William S. Lieberman

The American Federation of Arts

RIZZOLI
NEW YORK

The American Federation of Arts is a nonprofit art museum service organization that provides traveling art exhibitions and educational, professional, and technical support programs developed in collaboration with the museum community. Through these programs, the AFA seeks to strengthen the ability of museums to enrich the public's experience and understanding of art.

Published by The American Federation of Arts 41 East 65th Street, New York, NY 10021, and Rizzoli International Publications, Inc. 300 Park Avenue South New York, New York 10010

Library of Congress Cataloging-in-Publication Data

Metropolitan Museum of Art (New York, N.Y.)
    Still life : the object in American art, 1915–1995 : selections from the Metropolitan Museum of Art / Lowery Stokes Sims and Sabine Rewald.
        p.   cm.
    "American Federation of Arts."
    ISBN 0-8478-1982-5 (hardcover).—ISBN 1-885444-03-6 (pbk.)
    1. Still-life painting, American—Exhibitions. 2. Still-life painting—20th century—United States—Exhibitions.   3. Still-life painting—New York (State)—New York—Exhibitions. 4. Metropolitan Museum of Art (New York, N.Y.)—Exhibitions.   I. Sims, Lowery Stokes.   II. Rewald, Sabine.   III. Title.
ND1392.6.M48   1996
758'.4'09730747471—dc20
                                                        96-13235
                                                        CIP

Publication Coordinator, AFA: Michaelyn Mitchell
Editor: Brian Wallis
Designer: Russell Hassell
Photography: Photography Studio, The Metropolitan Museum of Art

Front cover: James Rosenquist, *Gift Wrapped Doll #16,* 1992 (cat. no. 66)
Frontispiece: Mark Tansey, *Still Life* (detail), 1982 (cat. no. 24)
Page 6: Samuel Halpert, *The Red Tablecloth* (detail), 1915 (cat. no. 39)

Printed in Singapore

This catalogue has been published in conjunction with *Still Life: The Object in American Art, 1915–1955—Selections from The Metropolitan Museum of Art*, an exhibition organized by The Metropolitan Museum of Art and The American Federation of Arts. It is made possible by a generous grant from Metropolitan Life Foundation. Additional support has been provided by the National Patrons of the AFA.

EXHIBITION ITINERARY

Marsh Art Gallery
Richmond, Virginia
January 3–February 28, 1997

The Arkansas Arts Center
Little Rock, Arkansas
March 28–May 23, 1997

Newport Harbor Art Museum
Newport Beach, California
June 20–August 15, 1997

Philbrook Museum of Art
Tulsa, Oklahoma
September 12–November 7, 1997

The Society of the Four Arts
Palm Beach, Florida
January 9–February 8, 1998

Salina Art Center
Salina, Kansas
March 6–May 3, 1998

Metropolitan Life Foundation is pleased to join The American Federation of Arts and The Metropolitan Museum of Art to bring you *Still Life: The Object in American Art, 1915–1995—Selections from The Metropolitan Museum of Art*. The exhibition and its accompanying catalogue highlight the vitality of the still-life paintings produced in this century. The sixty-six works are drawn from the collections of one of the preeminent museums in the world and present, through a variety of subjects, the different painting styles of over fifty artists. We are delighted to be part of this important project, which celebrates the richness of the American still-life tradition.

Harry P. Kamen
Chairman, President, and Chief Executive Officer
Metropolitan Life Insurance Company

CONTENTS

ACKNOWLEDGMENTS

Still Life: The Object in American Art, 1915–1995 is the sixth exhibition in an ongoing collaboration between the Metropolitan Museum of Art and the American Federation of Arts designed to share the museum's vast resources with other institutions around the country. Its presentation is timely. Just over thirty years ago the American Federation of Arts sponsored the exhibition *A Century of American Still Life Painting, 1813–1913*, organized by William H. Gerdts. At that time still-life painting was an overlooked category, a minor genre in comparison to portraiture, landscape and historical paintings, or religious and mythological subjects. Since then, there has been a steady reevaluation of still life, and the richness of the genre is demonstrated in this selection of sixty-six paintings from the twentieth century art collection at the Metropolitan Museum.

For their contributions to both the exhibition and this publication, we wish to thank the following staff members at the Metropolitan Museum: William S. Lieberman, Jacques and Natasha Gelman Chairman of 20th Century Art, and his colleagues, Lowery Stokes Sims, curator; Sabine Rewald, associate curator; Lisa Messinger, assistant curator; Ida Balboul, research associate; Alleyne Miller, administrative assistant; and present and former interns and fellows in the department, Brian Boucher, Akiko Hasekawa, Michele Marcantonio, Jessica Murphy, and Susan Rosenberg. We would like to acknowledge as well the contributions of Lucy Belloli of the Paintings Conservation Laboratory; Marceline McKee from the Loans Office; and Nestor Montilla in the Office of the Registrar.

We also thank those members of the AFA staff whose efforts have been important to the realization of this project: Marie-Thérèse Brincard, senior curator of exhibitions; Rachel Granholm, head of education; Alexandra Mairs, former exhibitions/publications assistant; Michaelyn Mitchell, head of publications; María Gabriela Mizes, registrar; Martha Neighbors, former exhibitions coordinator; Thomas Padon, director of exhibitions; and Jillian Slonim, director of public information.

We would like to acknowledge the participation of the presenting museums: the Marsh Art Gallery, Richmond, Virginia; The Arkansas Arts Center, Little Rock; the Newport Harbor Art Museum, Newport Beach, California; the Philbrook Museum of Art, Tulsa, Oklahoma; The Society of the Four Arts, Palm Beach, Florida; and the Salina Art Center, Salina, Kansas.

Lastly, we would like to thank the Metropolitan Life Foundation for their very generous support, without which the project would not have been possible, and the National Patrons of the AFA, who have designated this project as the National Patron Exhibition of 1997.

Philippe de Montebello
Director, The Metropolitan Museum of Art

Serena Rattazzi
Director, The American Federation of Arts

INTRODUCTION

LOWERY STOKES SIMS
AND SABINE REWALD

As recently as the early 1980s, still life was considered a minor genre. Despite its roots in the wall decorations of antiquity and its dramatic proliferation in Europe during the sixteenth and seventeenth centuries, still-life painting always suffered in comparison to the supposedly loftier genres of portraiture, landscape, history painting, and religious and mythological subjects. In the nascent American school of the eighteenth and nineteenth centuries, still-life painting was often dismissed for its lack of heroics and distrusted for its promotion of trompe l'oeil illusionism. Even with such influential practitioners as Caravaggio, Chardin, and Cézanne, still life remained for centuries the neglected stepchild of high art.

In the American art of the twentieth century, however, still-life painting has found a new relevance and respect. Within the context of modern art, the very premises and techniques that had governed the development of still life—spatial and formal illusionism and sumptuous rendering of surface—made it the perfect vehicle for an aggressive deconstruction of the surface, texture, and form of academic painting. And, in America, the spectacular rise of consumer society in the early years of this century only increased the attention that artists began to lavish on objects that had been primed and primped for consumption. As Linda Cathcart has noted,

American concern for objects has always been thought to be both a specific and somewhat native one. There is a love of the way things in this country look, and yet at the same time a resentment that these objects fill and obliterate the landscape. It is this obsession with objects which makes still life a natural, compelling subject for many American artists.[1]

FIG. 1   Jacques de Gheyn the Elder, *Vanitas Still Life*, 1603. Oil on wood, 32½ x 21¼ in. Charles B. Curtis, Marquand, Victor Wilbour Memorial, and The Alfred N. Punnett Endowment Funds, 1974 (1974.1)

In the mid-1960s, the American Federation of Arts began an important series of traveling exhibitions focusing on American still-life painting. This series included *A Century of American Still-Life Painting, 1813–1913* (1966) and *American Still-Life Painting, 1913–1967* (1967), both organized by William Gerdts, and *Still-Life Painting Today*, organized in 1971 in consultation with Tom L. Freudenheim, Martin L. Friedman, Lloyd McNeill, and Donald L. Weisman. Many of the artists featured in those earlier projects are also included in this survey of twentieth-century still-life paintings from the Metropolitan Museum of Art. Among these artists are Stuart Davis, Preston Dickinson, Samuel Halpert, Marsden Hartley, Walt Kuhn, Yasuo Kuniyoshi, Henry Lee McFee, Walter Murch, Georgia O'Keeffe, Bradley Walker Tomlin, Franklin Watkins, and Max Weber. What is different about this show, however, is that of the sixty-six works included over a third were created after 1980.

In fact, there was a surprising resurgence of interest in still-life painting in the 1980s. Exhibitions such as Frank H. Goodyear Jr.'s 1981 survey *Contemporary American Realism Since 1960* at the Pennsylvania Academy of the Fine Arts; Linda Cathcart's 1983 exhibition *American Still Life, 1945–1983* at the Contemporary Arts Museum, Houston; Dahlia Morgan's *American Art Today: Still Life* (1984) at the Art Museum,

Florida International University, Miami; Paula A. Foley and Zoltan Buki's *Contemporary American Still Life* shown at the New Jersey State Museum, Trenton, in 1986; and the 1994 survey *Still-life Painting,* organized by Karyn Esielonis at the Museum of Fine Arts, Boston, are important benchmarks of this revival. The Houston exhibition, in particular, prompted a wide range of critical responses.[2] This, in part, precipitated a number of revisionist art-historical views of still-life painting, most notably Norman Bryson's landmark study *Looking at the Overlooked: Four Essays on Still Life Painting,* published in 1990.[3]

Although the development of still-life painting in Europe and America cannot be completely told through examples of paintings in the Metropolitan Museum, the collection does include many notable still lifes. The earliest Western still-life painting in the museum's collection, *Vanitas Still Life* (fig. 1) by the Dutch painter Jacques de Gheyn the Elder (1565–1629), is in fact the earliest known depiction of the vanitas theme. The composition has great simplicity. The human skull sits in an alcove surrounded by the symbols of human vanities—a large soap bubble, a tulip, smoke, and coins.

The Netherlands provided the richest soil for still-life painting. These works were painted for, and acquired by, an appreciative bourgeoisie to decorate their houses. The museum owns the works of two painters who might be said to represent two styles fashionable at the time. Jan Brueghel the Younger (1601–1678) presents the "salon" still life with his jewel-like *A Basket of Flowers* (fig. 2). His Flemish contemporary Jan Fyt (1611–1661) creates the "kitchen" still life in images of dead partridges, hares, and birds.

When the French Jean Siméon Chardin (1731–1768) looked at Dutch still-life painting, he studied Fyt's rather than Brueghel's work. Chardin was the first great artist to paint still lifes of commonplace objects, usually food and kitchen utensils. The museum owns one early still life by Chardin, *The Silver Tureen* (fig. 3). In this painting, a curious cat studies a pewter soup tureen and a dead hare, and some apples are set against a dark background. What is striking about the work is its simplicity, especially if compared to *Still Life with Silver* (fig. 4) by Chardin's contemporary Alexandre François Desportes (1661–1743). Desportes's huge canvas presents a buffet

FIG. 2   Jan Brueghel the Younger, *A Basket of Flowers*. Oil on wood, 18 1/2 x 26 7/8 in. The Metropolitan Museum of Art, Bequest of Miss Adelaide Milton de Groot (1876–1967), 1967 (67.187.58)

FIG. 3   Jean Siméon Chardin, *The Silver Tureen*, ca. 1728. Oil on canvas, 30 x 42 1/2 in. The Metropolitan Museum of Art, Fletcher Fund, 1959 (59.9)

FIG. 4   Alexandre François Desportes, *Still Life with Silver*. Oil on canvas, 103 x 73 ¾ in. The Metropolitan Museum of Art, Purchase, Bequest of Mary Wetmore Shively in memory of her husband, Henry L. Shively, M.D., 1964 (64.315)

laden with valuable porcelain objects, silver vessels studded with semiprecious stones, and pyramids of rare and luscious fruits. Desportes overwhelms the viewer with opulence and painterly virtuosity while Chardin relies on understatement. Chardin's unique talent for arranging humble objects into something approaching poetry was recognized even by his contemporaries.

But the artist who learned most from Chardin was Paul Cézanne (1839–1906), who is said to have composed still life in an almost musical way. The artist's group of five still lifes in the museum's collection ranges from the modest *Apples* (1878–79) to the richly textured *Still Life with a Ginger Jar and Eggplants* (fig. 5). The latter abounds with the objects Cézanne made famous—Provençal fabrics, faience pieces, apples, olive jars, crumpled napkins and plaster casts—and that have been associated with him ever since. Other artists have also been identified with specific objects or elements they preferred for their still lifes. The French symbolist Odilon Redon (1840–1916), himself of fragile disposition, was fond of ethereal, dreamlike flowers. Such delicate and short-lived flowers as poppies, marigolds, or anemones appear in a group of the artist's pictures in the museum's collection.

Still life was the ideal vehicle for the spatial distortions and experiments Pablo Picasso and Georges Braque undertook in the development of cubism. Their ongoing influence remains evident in the still lifes of their French colleagues in the Metropolitan Museum, among them, André Derain's *The Table* (fig. 6), Jacques Villon's *The Dining Table* (1912) and Braque's later *The Gueridon* (1921–22).

Still-life painting in America had a glamorous beginning in the portraits by John Singleton Copley (1737–1815). These well-to-do Americans of the late eighteenth century proudly displayed their prosperity by posing with silver vessels or rich porcelain wares. In the early nineteenth century, the Peale family continued this tradition with startlingly realistic still lifes. The earliest American still life in the museum's collection is *Still Life with Cake* (fig. 7) by Raphaelle Peale (1774–1825), the son of the dynasty's founder, Charles Willson Peale (1741–1827). *Still Life with Cake,* a small image of iced raisin cake cut in quarters next to a claret-filled glass, is touching because of its subdued color and air of small-town propriety.

FIG. 5   Paul Cézanne, *Still Life with a Ginger Jar and Eggplants*, 1890. Oil on canvas, 28½ x 36 in. The Metropolitan Museum of Art, Bequest of Stephen C. Clark, 1960 (61.101.4)

FIG. 6   André Derain, *The Table*, 1911. Oil on canvas, 38 x 51⅝ in. The Metropolitan Museum of Art, Wolfe Fund, 1954. Catharine Lorillard Wolfe Collection (54.79)

FIG. 7   Raphaelle Peale, *Still Life with Cake*, 1818. Oil on wood, 10 ¾ x 15 ¼ in. The Metropolitan Museum of Art, Maria DeWitt Jesup Fund, 1959 (59.166)

The move from the depiction of nature's bounty to that of man-made objects was evident in the teasing trompe l'oeil paintings of the late nineteenth century. The museum is especially rich in works by William Michael Harnett (1848–1892) and his followers John F. Peto (1854–1907) and John Haberle (1856–1933). Harnett's *The Artist's Letter Rack* (fig. 8) shows a grid of pink tape with a selection of envelopes, cards, and other papers rendered in textures that simulate their actual materials, and that are meant to delight and show off the artist's virtuosity.

In Marsden Hartley's *Portrait of a German Officer* (fig. 9), figures, initials, medals, badges, tassels, and military insignia are combined in one of the earliest abstractions conceived by an American artist. This abstract still life, painted in Berlin at the beginning of World War I, commemorated the death of Hartley's handsome German friend. Male friendship is also celebrated in Charles Demuth's *The Figure 5 in Gold* (fig. 10), which pays homage to the artist's close friend poet William Carlos Williams. The title of the painting comes from Williams's poem "The Great Figure," and, as in a cubist collage, the jumble of numbers, initials, lights, and colors attempts to recreate the poem's description of a fire engine speeding through the night.

Over the centuries, one of the most compelling aspects of still-life painting was the consistency of its compositional elements and their interpretation. For a number of reasons, this dependability has been broken down radically in the twentieth century. As mass-produced objects proliferated on the American scene, for instance, they provided an expanded repertoire of images, whose symbolic decoding lay in the personality and predilections of the artist rather than in the more public realms of religion or civics. While the flowers, fruits, and china in many of the compositions in this exhibition conform to historical precedents, works like Walter Murch's *Isotope* (cat. no. 48) more accurately typify the jarring and somewhat anomalous character of many twentieth-century still lifes. Thus, even though, the genesis of the Murch work (which depicts a mechanical apparatus used to handle radioactive materials) was a rather prosaic illustration assignment for a magazine, his isolation of the objects against a dramatically illuminated background removes this object from its usual context and creates a dissonance between its identity and the artist's mode of representation. Here, truth is not in the materials.

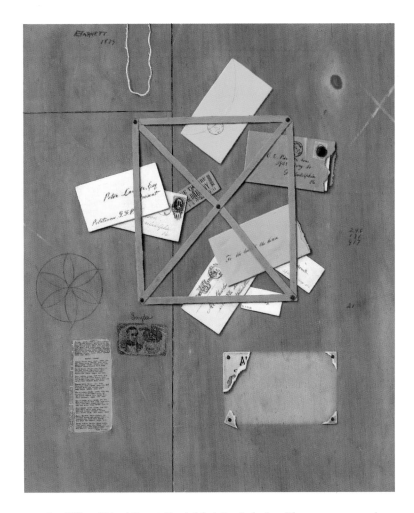

FIG. 8   William Michael Harnett, *The Artist's Letter Rack*, 1879. Oil on canvas, 30 x 25 in. The Metropolitan Museum of Art, Morris K. Jesup Fund, 1966 (66.13)

FIG. 9   Marsden Hartley, *Portrait of a German Officer*, 1914. Oil on canvas, 68 1/4 x 41 3/8 in. The Metropolitan Museum of Art, The Alfred Stieglitz Collection, 1949 (49.70.42)

This new attitude toward still life can also be distinguished by the specific relationship that is established between the will to depict and the act of painting. As critic Barry Schwabsky has pointed out, despite the assumption that still-life painting was abandoned with the rise of abstraction in American art during the period between the two world wars, still life was in fact central to that development. Stuart Davis, a key figure in that revolution, broke through to pure abstraction by combining cubism and surrealism in his *Eggbeater* paintings of 1927–28. These works featured arrangements of unexpected combinations, such as an eggbeater, a rubber glove, and a fan. For the ten years prior to the *Eggbeater* paintings, Davis had consistently returned to the object as a means to exploring modernist idioms. His *Studio Interior* of 1917 (cat. no. 26) is an early use of objects as surrogates for portraiture. His 1924 study of an electric light bulb (cat. no. 40) brings still life squarely into the twentieth century, contrasting the world of the past (the glass goblet) with that of the present (the incandescent light bulb).

Georgia O'Keeffe's *Corn, Dark I* (cat. no. 1), also painted in 1924, is a marvel of mixed metaphors, alluding to both abstraction and reality and to both landscape and plant forms. It demonstrates what Lisa Messinger has called the "emotive power" of form. A. E. Gallatin carried O'Keeffe's reduction of form to an extreme in his 1940 *Number 28 (Still Life)* (cat. no. 45). Here, the shapes are so abstract and anonymous that it is impossible to assign any fixed identity to them. The paintings of Karl Knaths (cat. no. 22), Carlyle Brown (cat. no. 49), and Lee Gatch (cat. no. 5) show how American artists continued to be indebted to late cubism (Knaths and Gatch) and surrealism (exemplified by the dreamlike reverie of Brown's *Table with Figs and Lemons*).

These works provide a potent rebuttal to the theory that still-life painting was superseded by abstract expressionism. In fact, many American artists of the period were vocal opponents of abstraction. And, what is less often acknowledged, still-life painting played a fundamental role in the evolution of many artists associated with abstract expressionism. Franz Kline's early *Still Life with Puppet* (cat. no. 46) and Bradley Walker Tomlin's *Burial* (cat. no. 4), for instance, reveal aspects of these artists' later abstract work: in Kline's case, it is the gestural approach to painting, while for Tomlin it is the incisive exploration of forms as spatial devices. Ironically, though, David Smith's preternaturally gestural abstraction of a *Seashell and Map* (cat. no. 2) provides the clearest example of gestural painting as a personal mode of depiction.

FIG. 10   Charles Henry Demuth, *The Figure 5 in Gold*, 1928. Oil on composition board, 36 x 29¾ in. The Metropolitan Museum of Art, Alfred Stieglitz Collection, 1949 (49.59.1)

Pop art has had a significant influence on recent American art, particularly in relation to the presentation of the object. With its blatant replication of consumer products and packaging, this movement extended the surrealist approach to the object into a method for producing revelations that were as poetic as they were polemic. In James Rosenquist's *House of Fire* (fig. 11), for example, he revives the surrealist notion of visual displacement, creating a juxtaposition as jarring as Comte de Lautréamont's famous "chance encounter of a sewing machine and an umbrella on a dissection table." On three huge panels, Rosenquist depicts a collision between

FIG. 11   James Rosenquist, *House of Fire*, 1981. Oil on canvas, 78 x 198 in. The Metropolitan Museum of Art, Purchase, George A. and Arthur Hoppock Hearn Funds and Lila Acheson Wallace Gift, 1982 (1982.90.1a-c)

three symbols of American life: a grocery bag turned on its head (domesticity); a molten steel bucket (industry); and an army of giant lipsticks (consumerism).

The pop artists' use of photographic and other commercial printing processes also helped to create a dramatic transformation in the conventional distinction between illusion and actuality. This exhibition includes several recent examples of the work of key figures: Andy Warhol's

Still Life (cat. no. 59), Rosenquist's *Gift Wrapped Doll #16* (cat. no. 66), and Jim Dine's *The Heart, South of Naples* (cat. no. 61). While the Warhol is a subtle play on Communist symbology in American consumer goods, the Rosenquist appropriates a close-up image of a plastic-covered doll's head to make a statement about AIDS. Dine's heraldic presentation of a heart, surrounded by marine life, extends the artist's exploration of that symbol as a metaphor for personal emotions and relationships. Beyond such paradigmatic works, subtler vestiges of pop-inflected imagery can be discerned

in the insistent attention to packaging and labels in Paul Wonner's *"Dutch" Still Life with Orchids, Postcard View of Paris, and "Death of Marat"* (cat. no. 53) and in Randall Deihl's display of store-bought confections (cat. no. 35). The intense physicality and pristinely photographic character of Audrey Flack's *Macarena of Miracles* (cat. no. 58) also demonstrates the affinities between pop art and photorealism.

Studies of still-life painting have tended to define a more or less constant number of categories. These include: table-top compositions, interior scenes, and still lifes in nature. The first category may be broken down further into floral and or fruit studies, harvest and/or hunt paintings, as well as table settings. Where the composition is meant to have more symbolic content, the descriptions may include the moralistic categorizations of "vanitas," "memento mori," and the like. "Trompe l'oeil," "objectivism," and "botanical" are later terms from the nineteenth century that describe technical approaches to the subject matter (e.g., illusionistic techniques and scientific examination or description). Stylistic movements can also be singled out (for example, the use of "machine" imagery or precisionism in the 1920s and '30s).[4] In certain cases, even heraldic portraits of animals can form a category of still life.

The six categories of still-life painting developed for this exhibition—"Still Life and the Landscape," "Harvests, Hunts, and Bountiful Settings," "Flower Paintings," "Interiors and Genre Scenes," "Table Still Life," and "The Iconic Object"—correspond to the nature of the paintings selected and to the numerical representations of works in each category. "The Iconic Object," for instance, includes works that present a single image or object as the focus of the composition. These paintings provide a context within which to present objects shown out of context. Many paintings could belong to more than one of the categories; some works included in the sections "Flower Paintings" and "Harvests, Hunts, and Bountiful Settings" could just as easily have been added to the category "Table Still Life."

While the selection of works for this exhibition does not include sculpture, works on paper, or photography, artists have created strong images in these mediums over the last century.[5] Photography, in particular, has shaped the reception and perception of the object in modern art and in still-life painting. The work of photographers such as Edward Weston, Paul Strand, Imogen Cunningham, Paul Outerbridge, and Charles Sheeler, to name a few, has precipitated a vibrant cross-fertilization between painting and photography that has revolutionized the notion of still life.

Sculpture by artists such as Jim Dine and Claes Oldenburg employed everyday objects and consumer items in sculptural forms to declare the importance of the ordinary and the familiar. Undoubtedly, as we move into the twenty-first century, artists will engage technologies such as holography and virtual reality to further transform our notions of still life. In the meantime, the work presented in this exhibition amply affirms the current and continuing vitality of this genre in contemporary art.

1 Linda L. Cathcart, *American Still Life, 1945–1983*, exhib. cat. (Houston: Contemporary Arts Museum, 1983), 28.
2 See, notably, Eric Gibson, "American Still Life," *New Criterion* (October 1984): 70–73; and Barry Schwabsky, "Is There Still Life in Still Life," *Arts Magazine* (November 1984): 130–32.
3 Norman Bryson, *Looking at the Overlooked: Four Essays on Still Life Painting* (Cambridge, Mass.: Harvard University Press, 1990).
4 See Wolfgang Born, *Still-Life Painting in America*. (New York: Oxford University Press, 1947), and Carter Radcliff's essay in *American Art Today: Still Life,* exhib. cat. (Miami: The Art Museum at Florida International University, 1985).
5 These categories were included in the exhibition *Contemporary New England Still Life,* organized in 1984 by the De Cordova Museum and Dana Museum and Park in Lincoln, Massachusetts.

CATALOGUE

STILL LIFE AND THE LANDSCAPE

Botanical studies constitute one of the principal categories of still-life painting. A particular manifestation of nineteenth-century American painting, botanical studies are characterized by their focus on the scientific observation of nature. They are distinguished from the broader category of landscape painting by their use of what critic Raquel Da Rosa has called the "essential gesture" of still-life painting—the isolation of objects in the world.[1] This gesture is demonstrated in the extreme close-up of a white rose in Jennifer Bartlett's *One A.M.* (cat. no. 10). Within the floral bounty of this view of the artist's New York garden from the early 1990s, this one blossom, fully extended and just out of reach, beckons the viewer.

According to art historian Wolfgang Born, the botanical still life was invented by the nineteenth-century American painter Rubens Peale.[2] Almost a century later, Audrey Buller enlisted the dead stump of a tree to serve as a receptacle for the effusive growth of her *Morning Glory* (cat. no. 3). This composition, set at the eye level of a small animal, enhances our intimate view of the flowers, which seem monumental against the backdrop of a tiny townscape and mountains across the lake. In fact, many of the paintings in this section feature still-life elements or setups seen in relationship to a distant view, often seen through a window. Jane Freilicher frequently makes such juxtapositions in her work. The Manhattan skyline forms a backdrop to a tabletop still life in her *Bread and Bricks* (cat. no. 8). And Freilicher's *The Lute Player* (cat. no. 11) combines an appropriate vignette from Jean-Antoine Watteau's eighteenth-century painting *Mezzetin* (ca. 1718–20, Metropolitan Museum of Art) with a contemporary view of the flatlands of Long Island.

In Lee Gatch's *The Thorn* (cat. no. 5) a still-life arrangement of the utensils of the Last Supper are seen against a view of the three crosses of the Crucifixion outside on a hilltop. Similarly, in Jonathan Weinberg's *The Wheel, St. Catherine* (cat. no. 6), the instrument of the saint's torture, set in a modern-day locale on New York City's West Side, is seen against a cityscape outside the window. In Bradley Walker Tomlin's dreamlike composition *Burial* (cat. no. 4), exterior and interior seem to coexist in a manner that transcends time and space.

The centrally placed blue blanket in Catherine Murphy's deceptively simple composition (cat. no. 9) owes as much to minimalist painting—in which an anonymous shape is set against a background—as it does to contemporary narrative. It is easy to imagine the scene as a prelude to a picnic al fresco or to a romantic encounter in nature. The center of Terry Allen's *The Prisoner's Song* (cat. no. 7) is dominated by an abstracted landscape, seen literally within a window. Allen has also set up individual "incidents" by collaging onto the surface of the painting drawings by Navajo men—all veterans of the Vietnam War and all incarcerated at one time or another. A text inscribed onto the lead surface of the painting articulates the cultural alienation suggested in the drawings.   L S S

1 Raquel Da Rosa, "Manet and the Modernist Still Life," in *Natura Naturata (An Argument for Still Life)*, exhib. cat. (New York: Josh Baer Gallery, 1989), n.p.
2 Wolfgang Born, *Still Life Painting in America* (New York: Oxford University Press, 1947), 11–12.

I   GEORGIA O'KEEFFE   *Corn, Dark I,* 1924

Georgia O'Keeffe's work is distinguished by a sensitivity to the innate, emotive power of form.[1] In this representation of a corn plant, the compositional elements are arranged along a vertical axis, an arrangement that is emphasized by the searing slit of the light on the shiny leaves. The plant is seen at close range, allowing no sense of its overall form. Its broad, dark green leaves are set against a purple background, but the focal point of the composition is a curious circle of lapis blue just below the midpoint.

O'Keeffe's sense of line and color comes not only from her own intuitive artistic sensibility but also from her familiarity with the creative philosophy of Arthur Wesley Dow, with whom she studied at the Teachers College of Columbia University from 1915 to 1916. "Dow taught that through the artist's selective orchestration of format and composition elements each subject's true identity could be revealed," notes art historian Lisa Messinger.[2] But, lest the viewer try to read arcane metaphysical symbolism into O'Keeffe's work, it is important to note that her representation of a corn plant is based on solid empirical observation.

In the summer of 1924, while visiting Lake George (where her future husband, Alfred Stieglitz, was also vacationing with his family), O'Keeffe cultivated a garden. She later recalled:

The growing corn was one of my special interests, the light-colored veins of the dark green leaves reaching out in opposite directions. And every morning a little drop of dew would have run down the veins into the center of this plant like a little lake all fine and fresh.[3]

Corn, Dark I is one of three variations on a study of corn plants that O'Keeffe produced that summer. It is also the most essential, eschewing the floridness of the subsequent paintings. Her close attention to the most minute features of the plant indicates the degree to which, at this point in her career, O'Keeffe was engaged with the philosophical views of Arthur Dove, an associate of the Stieglitz circle. In the 1920s, Dove developed his signature style based on the distillation of natural phenomena. LSS

1 Lisa Mintz Messinger, *Georgia O'Keeffe* (New York and London: Thames and Hudson and the Metropolitan Museum of Art, 1988), 13.
2 Ibid.
3 Ibid., 32.

Seashell and Map by the sculptor David Smith was inspired by an extended trip to the Virgin Islands. Smith and his first wife, sculptor Dorothy Dehner, spent eight months there in 1931 and 1932. Art historian Edward Fry has claimed that this sojourn was a watershed in Smith's artistic evolution, since, during that time, he "clarified [his] previously tentative efforts to translate European modernism into the vernacular of American experience."[1] The focus of this painting is the large brown form outlined in yellow with an area of crosshatching literally scratched into the surface of the paint. This seems to represent the flattened, abstracted image of a large conch shell, a familiar souvenir of the Caribbean. The strange green forms behind the shell, as well as the salmon field and the dark brown borders at the right and left, resemble "those on a map that describe the contours of land and water."[2] The combination of the shell and the map recalls certain typical Dutch still-life compositions from the seventeenth and eighteenth centuries.

Smith's composition, with its large central form, can be compared with Georgia O'Keeffe's *Clam Shell* (cat. no. 57), painted three years earlier. The pristine quality of the O'Keeffe is informed by modernist photography, in which the close scrutiny of the object—no manner how humble—creates a new awareness of its meaning and abstract qualities. In the Smith painting, the working of the surface seems to take precedence, as evidenced by the aggressively gestural paint handling. Also, Smith's sense of form is purposely evocative rather than specific. Smith once noted, "I belong with painters, in a sense; all my early friends were painters because we all studied together. And I never conceived of myself as anything other than a painter because my work came right through the raised surface and color and objects applied to the surface."[3] This bridge between his painting and his sculpture can be seen here in Smith's particular approach to texture and the accumulation of forms. His interests in cubism, constructivism, and surrealism are evident, and the yellow, brown, green, and salmon tonalities suggest the works of Georges Braque from the 1920s and 1930s.

It is interesting to note that Smith made his first completely sculptural works from coral and wire while he was in the Virgin Islands. The collection of shells and rocks that he brought back to New York in 1932 was later incorporated into other sculptures. These became the harbingers of his mature work, in which individual still-life objects are combined in poetic associations. LSS

1 Edward Fry, "David Smith, An Appreciation," in *David Smith,* exhib. cat. (New York: Solomon R. Guggenheim Museum, 1969), 10.
2 Lisa Mintz Messinger, in *Notable Acquisitions, 1983–84* (New York: Metropolitan Museum of Art, 1984), 94.
3 David Smith, interview with David Sylvester, June 6, 1961, in *David Smith: Paintings from the 1930s,* exhib. cat. (New York: Washburn Gallery, 1987), n.p.

A native of Montreal, Audrey Buller was the daughter of a prominent professor of ophthalmology at McGill University. Buller's two older sisters were also artists; one of them, Cecil, was a distinguished printmaker, admired for her wood engravings that skillfully adapted modernist idioms. Buller was educated in England, and studied art at the Art Gallery of Montreal under the renowned Canadian painter Randolph Hewton. In the 1920s she emigrated to New York, where she enrolled in the Art Students League and attended classes taught by Kenneth Hayes Miller and Henry Schnakenberg. By the early 1930s, she was showing in New York at both the Rehn Gallery and the Feragil Galleries, where this painting was acquired in 1938. Buller exhibited in the Third Biennial Exhibition of Contemporary American Painting at the Whitney Museum of American Art (1936), the Annual Exhibition at the National Academy of Design (1938), and the Carnegie International (1939). She also exhibited on several occasions during the 1940s in the Annual Exhibition of the Pennsylvania Academy of the Fine Arts, and was the recipient of several awards, including the Proctor Portrait Prize from the National Academy of Design and a prize in an exhibition sponsored by the Pepsi-Cola Company in 1945.

In his 1951 survey of American art, art historian John I. H. Baur noted Buller's work, along with that of Katherine Schmidt and John Rogers Cox, as exemplars of a strain of "hard, Immaculate-related realism."[1] In particular, Baur praised Buller's work for "its rectilinear design and spare simplicity,"[2] characteristics that are evident in this curious composition of a petunia vine. The orderly swirl of the petunia blossoms as they emerge from a tree stump (which functions as a vase) contrasts with the more haphazard pile of dried, insect-ravaged leaves on the ground.

Buller's careful rendering of the individual leaves and blossoms of the vine follows a well-established tradition of botanical still-life painting, rooted in nineteenth-century American art. The philosophical objectivism that often characterized the earlier work can be seen in the detached, illustrative nature of Buller's image. In addition, the extreme close-up view of the flowers, which fill the front plane of this composition, is reminiscent of the unusual organization and spatial techniques of trompe l'oeil painters. In the far distance of Buller's work, a tiny landscape with gentle, rolling hills stretches beneath a wide expanse of sky. The only hint of human presence is the cluster of buildings at the lower left, a spired church and a mill or factory building. LSS

1 John I. H. Baur, *Revolution and Tradition in Modern American Art* (Cambridge, Mass.: Harvard University Press, 1951), 104.
2 Ibid.

Bradley Walker Tomlin, a man of delicate health and refined sensibilities, has been described as looking like an impoverished aristocrat. "One would have thought he was the son of an Anglican bishop," said Robert Motherwell. "But he loved painters and paintings, this is the essential fact about him."[1] Tomlin was born in Syracuse, New York, and studied art at Syracuse University. In the 1920s, he worked as an illustrator, designing magazine covers for *Vogue* and *House and Garden*. Although he lived in Paris between 1923 and 1924, his letters home reveal a growing impatience with Left Bank bohemian life and a blissful unawareness of works by contemporary artists such as Picasso, Braque, or Matisse. Instead, Tomlin chose to study works of Cézanne, van Gogh, and Gauguin.

After his return from Europe, Tomlin was for years swayed by the influence of other artists and was unable to forge a distinctive style of his own. His paintings vacillated between a softened realism and a half-hearted cubism. The pivotal event in Tomlin's career was the exhibition *Fantastic Art, Dada, Surrealism* at the Museum of Modern Art in 1936. According to art historian John I. H. Baur, although "Tomlin was deeply repelled at first, he kept returning [to the exhibition] with fascination, finally confessing that other art began to look dull in comparison."[2] Thereafter, Tomlin began to incorporate symbolic and fragmentary elements into his cubist compositions, of which *Burial* is a typical example. The subdued, earthy coloring and the softly blurred outlines create an atmosphere in which fragments of architecture and statuary seem suspended. The mood is dreamy, yet the spatial relationships are precise and complex. Among the abstract elements that are superimposed on the underlying geometric grid are a variety of architectural fragments and a classical bust crowned by a green laurel wreath.

Tomlin painted this group of cubist still lifes mainly during World War II. Their muted, elegiac mood and suggestive titles reflect the hardships of war time. At the end of the war, Tomlin formed a close attachment to Adolph Gottlieb, who introduced him to Jackson Pollock, Philip Guston, Willem de Kooning, and Motherwell. Tomlin's association with these artists led him toward an individual and highly lyrical version of abstract expressionism—large abstract paintings animated by ribbonlike calligraphic marks—the style for which he is most celebrated today. S R

1 Jeanne Chenault Porter, "Introduction," *Bradley Walker Tomlin, 1899–1953: Paintings*, exhib. cat. (New York: Baruch College Gallery, 1989), n.p.
2 John I. H. Baur, *Bradley Walker Tomlin* (New York: Macmillan, 1957), 25.

5   LEE GATCH   *The Thorn*, 1953

Lee Gatch is said to have found his artistic vocation as a youth, when he came upon a drawing of a woman's head on a plaster wall in an abandoned house in the Maryland woods. "To see something actually drawn by hand suddenly thrilled him," writes art historian Perry Rathbone.[1] Born just outside Baltimore in 1902, Gatch studied art at the Maryland Institute College of Art in Baltimore, where his teachers included Leon Kroll and John Sloan. In his early twenties Gatch won a fellowship to study art in Paris. There, he enrolled in a private class taught by cubist painter André Lhote. He also admired the work of Pierre Bonnard and Paul Klee.

Gatch first showed his abstract landscapes in the United States in the 1930s, when social realism and surrealism were the prevailing styles and abstract art was still suspect. His lyrical abstractions quickly attracted a number of important collectors, including Duncan Phillips, who later founded the Phillips Collection in Washington, D.C. *The Thorn* shows Gatch's distinctive use of light and his lively handling of painterly surfaces, which Rathbone describes as "thin, dry areas of canvas contrasted with thick tactile licks of the brush and . . . fat palette knife work."[2] On first glance this painting seems to represent simply a table still life in front of an open window. But closer scrutiny reveals that these everyday elements relate symbolically to the Passion of Christ, the events leading up to his crucifixion.

On the table are a pitcher and a bread basket; next to them is a circle of thorns with a cross laid over it. Their predominantly purple hues reinforce the association with Christ's Passion. In the distance are shadowy outlines of the three crosses on which Christ and the two thieves were executed. The vertical member of the central cross descends into the interior space and terminates in the basket on the table. During the Last Supper, Christ gave bread and wine to the Apostles as symbols of his body and blood. Here, Gatch makes a visual connection between the body of Christ on the cross outside and the bread of life on the table.

At the extreme left of the painting is a large chalice. An arching band reaches from the mouth of the chalice across the window to the right of the composition. Within the trajectory of this band are representations of the moon in its various phases (including one where it blazes like the sun). This course traces the onset of darkness, referred to in the New Testament, that occurred as Christ was hung on the cross. When such religious imagery began to appear in Gatch's work in the mid-1940s, the waning moon was one of his favorite subjects, symbolizing the passage from life to death.[3]   LSS

1 Perry T. Rathbone, *Lee Gatch*, exhib. cat. (New York: American Federation of Arts, 1960), n.p.
2 Ibid.
3 Ibid.

New York artist Jonathan Weinberg is a romantic, something that is perhaps an anomaly in today's irony-laden art world. In the early nineteenth century, romantics turned to Gothic ruins for picturesque motifs. Similarly, searching for comparable, modern-day motifs, Weinberg prowled the abandoned piers along the West Side Highway in lower Manhattan in the early 1980s. "I have a kind of nostalgia for areas of the city that are in decay," he says.[1] One of the results of this fascination for defunct parts of the city was a large series of works showing dilapidated piers and other structures from unusual vantage points. Bereft of roofs and masonry, the rusted iron skeletons of these formerly bustling commercial buildings provided Weinberg with spectacular graphic effects. In *The Wheel, St. Catherine*, tall windows offer a view toward an abandoned building on the pier. Beyond the metal lattice of the broken window frame are an old two-story facade and two red brick smokestacks atop a power plant on West 12th Street. The large spiky wheel that gives the work its title is inside, resting on the window sill.

How did St. Catherine's wheel get to the Hudson Pier? While painting the "Pier" series, Weinberg was invited to participate in a group exhibition titled *Saints* at the Harm Bouckaert Gallery in New York in September 1983. Well aware that his current series of urban landscapes did not quite fit the theme of the exhibition, Weinberg decided to treat the subject symbolically. "Instead of trying to actually paint a saint, " he says, "I chose to paint Catherine's attribute, and thus suggest her presence in a modern environment."[2] Weinberg scavenged this particular wheel from an old bicycle but it is as transparent and as threatening as the one depicted in Caravaggio's famous painting of St. Catherine (ca. 1597, Collection Thyssen-Bornemisza, Lugano-Castagnola).

While the idea of displacing the saint's wheel to a gritty contemporary dock might seem farfetched, Weinberg sees a link between the sadomasochism involved in St. Catherine's torture and that of the homosexual encounters then taking place on the decaying piers. The chains hanging in the upper right of the cell-like interior point to this underlying narrative.

Today, the artist focuses on the derelict Times Square area. He deliberately works in a style that he calls "out of fashion" and "nostalgic." But his penchant for grids, areas of flatness, and vibrant colors also constitutes an homage to Weinberg's idol, Marsden Hartley. S R

1 Jonathan Weinberg, conversation with author, August 15, 1995. An assistant professor in the Department of the History of Literature at Yale University, Weinberg has written about and organized exhibitions on gay themes in art history. 2 Ibid.

7   TERRY ALLEN   *The Prisoner Song,* 1984

Terry Allen's interests in art, music, theater, and literature are all indicated in this multi-media painting in which several narrative modes are set out in separate acts across the picture plane. While some elements of this work may be described as realist, Allen introduces an episode of gestural abstraction within the central window which looks out on the world and which anchors the composition. The subject matter of the painting concerns the situation of Native American veterans of the Vietnam War, a focal point for Allen's work in the 1980s. The overlay of references to the war in Vietnam and the social, economic, and political condition of Native Americans results in a composition that is rich in allusion and daunting in its implications. Allen's approach to this material is uncompromising. He refuses to shirk the circumstances and consequences of history or to accommodate any sentimentalizing of that history.

In a small drawing at the upper left of the painting, a warrior attempts to capture an eagle—the most potent Native American symbol of freedom—by binding its talons. The bird's fierce resistance is indicated by the number of feathers it has lost in the struggle, Allen has also attached an actual feather to the painting surface just below the drawing. Other drawings affixed to the painting show a Native American warrior dressed in U.S. cavalry gear and another holding a bottle of alcohol and smoking a cigarette.

The words and texts that overlay the composition are set to a cadence that evokes traditional Native American chants. These phrases play a key role in illuminating the meaning of the picture. "Go to Jail / Draw Some Picture," for instance, refers to the central window space and to the pencil stubs dispersed across the picture plane. The tedium of incarceration is expressed by the phrase "Gum on the Wall" and the scratchings that mark the passage of time. "Fields of Fire" alludes to both the battlefields of Vietnam and traditional techniques for clearing land for planting. Historical sites are also referred to in the texts. These include Hue, Qia Ho, Citadel, Rivers of Perfume, and Saigon.[1]

The drawings in this painting were actually done by four Navaho Vietnam veterans while incarcerated in Gallup, New Mexico. Their subjects and the circumstances of their creation are reminiscent of the so-called ledger drawings that were executed by Native Americans from the Great Plains of the north-central United States, while confined in Florida from 1878 to 1885.[2]   LSS

1 Cited in Craig Adcock, *Kachina Hight: Terry Allen,* exhib. cat. (Tallahassee: Florida State University Fine Arts Gallery, 1986), 29–30.
2 See Julia Szabo, *Howling Wolf and the History of Ledger Art* (Albuquerque: University of New Mexico Press, 1994).

THE PRISONER SONG

HUE

GIA HO

CITADEL

RIVER OF PERFUME

SAIGON

START DEAD CENTER
ROB A TOOTH TOTEM

RUN TO THE LAKE
SHOOT UP AND DANCE

FUCK THE COPS
FLIP THEM THE BIRD

GO TO JAIL
DRAW COMIC PICTURES

LOOK AT THE WINDOW
LOOK OUT THE WORLD

WRITE HER A LETTER
PUT GUM ON THE WALL

TEAR OFF YOUR DICK

GOUGE OUT YOUR EYES

SWEETEN THE FIELDS OF FIRE

This composition consists of what the artist describes as a "random grouping": forsythia in a porcelain pitcher, a ruler, two rolls and a loaf of bread, a wrapped package, and two buff-colored firebricks arranged on a table in the artist's studio. As is her custom, Freilicher has posed her still life against an outside view. Here, the skyline of Manhattan provides the backdrop, establishing a locale and affirming the contemporaneity of the moment. The branches of forsythia (the perennial herald of spring) stand out in this scene, with their yellow blooms and green leaves emerging from a blue-rimmed white porcelain pitcher. Freilicher's light-filled space indicates her affinities with impressionism, something she shared with friend and supporter Fairfield Porter.

While much still-life painting offers a vignette for contemplation, Freilicher seems to invite the spectator to partake of and touch the items on the table. Critic Klaus Kertess has described the elements in Freilicher's paintings as "surprised . . . before a clear pose of configuration could settle into a firm composition."[1] In this case, the surface of the table is tilted slightly upward, reorienting the perspective (a sensation that is subtly violated by the rendering of the pitcher of forsythia). Many descriptive details have been suppressed in favor of a concentration on the chromatic values in the painting, which play on an overall palette of earth tones: terracottas, maroons, mauves, browns, and beiges.

Freilicher studied art at Brooklyn College in the 1940s but was dissatisfied with the school's Bauhaus-oriented curriculum. She found an alternative in Hans Hofmann's private painting classes in Manhattan. This training in the era of abstract expressionism is revealed in her current working methods. As she describes it, she quickly lays out a "hazy notion of what will be," then continues to work on the image, building it "gradually and purposefully."[2] The boldness of her strokes has elicited references not only to the work of Hofmann and Porter but also to that of Willem de Kooning, an artist whom Freilicher particularly admires.[3] LSS

1 Klaus Kertess, *Painting Horizons*, exhib. cat. (Southampton, N.Y.: Parrish Art Museum, 1989), n.p.
2 Margaret Mathews, "Jane Freilicher," *American Artist* (March 1983): 37.
3 Ibid.

9   CATHERINE MURPHY   *Blue Blanket,* 1990

This blue blanket evokes a pool of water animated by dappled sunlight or a piece of sky that has dropped to the earth. The idea for *Blue Blanket* came to Catherine Murphy in a dream.[1] She saw herself spreading a blanket for a picnic. Upon waking, she looked in a chest for a similar blanket and found the cerulean blue one that she used in this painting. Murphy spread the blanket on the slope of her front yard in Hyde Park, New York. Then, every sunny afternoon from early May until October for the next two years she painted this motif. After each day's work she would neatly fold the blanket and stow it away. On the next sunny afternoon she would carefully replace it on the exact spot, which she had plotted on the ground with markers.

The artist's method of painting outdoor motifs demonstrates that, just like the impressionists, she is dependent on the weather and sunlight for the color and topography of her work. However, unlike those earlier artists, Murphy is painstakingly precise in painting even the smallest detail, such as the leaves of the ground ivy in *Blue Blanket*. Because of her meticulous rendering of such details, her pictures look nearly photographic. In the case of *Blue Blanket*, she was interested in the cool abstract pattern created by the sunlight on the blanket, and its juxtaposition with the succulent, precisely rendered green leaves of ivy. Also, as Murphy had begun to remove the horizons from her landscapes, she wanted in this work to bring "the sky into the picture metaphorically."[2]

Since the artist began to exhibit her work in the early 1970s, she has focused on what might be called "artless" subjects. Murphy has been credited with making memorable paintings "out of almost nothing at all: a green garden-hose coiled up in the snow, or a close-up view of a window frame with peeling paint."[3] Such paintings echo the modest, self-contained life she and her husband, sculptor Harry Roseman, have pursued in places such as Jersey City, New Jersey; Madison, Kentucky; and, since 1979, Hyde Park. Since she likes to paint from where she lives, her "landscapes" are often unprepossessing urban or suburban views. They frequently look through windows, across neighboring rooftops, houses, or backyards. These vignettes evoke a homespun, suburban way of life, with its ubiquitous hedges, garden furniture, barbecues, and garages. Ingeniously, Murphy draws this small-town America into her plain and functional interiors through reflections in mirrors and shiny utilitarian objects. S R

1 Catherine Murphy, conversation with author, July 7, 1995.
2 Ibid.
3 John Russell, *New York Times,* November 10, 1989, C 28 (review).

Jennifer Bartlett's career forms a bridge between the formalist orientation of American art in the 1960s and the return to figuration in the 1980s. When Bartlett's work first gained attention in the 1970s, it featured an approach to image making that was conceptual and improvisational, exploiting the more decorative aspects of serial imagery. Bartlett translated elemental signs for houses and landscape details into a vocabulary of grids and geometric forms; these were then rendered on individual, brightly colored metal tiles. By the mid-1980s, however, Bartlett was involved in full-blown painterly figuration, even though she continued to work in series and to draw on conceptual and minimalist practices as the structural basis for her work.

One A.M. is part of a twenty-four painting cycle, titled "Air," which Bartlett worked on between 1991 and 1992. "Air" is one of four series planned by the artist to deal with the four elements. (She worked on "Fire" in the 1980s and completed "Earth" in 1994–95.) Each painting in the "Air" series represents an event or vignette from a different hour of a typical day (starting at 8 A.M.) in the artist's life. Each of the paintings is seven feet square and includes two grid elements: the underlying color grid and an overlay of plaid patterning. A clock in each composition indicates the time, giving the painting its title. Here, the artist chronicles the nocturnal wanderings of the figure silhouetted against the window at the right. He or she seems to have just paused to consider the garden outside.

Although this scene might seem to qualify more readily as a landscape painting, there are ample precedents for still lifes in "natural settings" (see, for example, *Morning Glory* by Audrey Buller [cat. no. 3]).[1] Here, Bartlett has created a hermetic oasis within an urban environment, where the focal point is not only the garden but also the white roses. Bartlett has lavished particular attention on the large, fully extended blossom at the upper left, which leans out from its branch, beckoning, just beyond arm's reach. In this one rose, Bartlett captures the spirit of earlier botanical still lifes, in which the artist not only engaged in a scientific scrutiny of specimens but also in the sheer enjoyment of nature's bounty. LSS

1 See *Contemporary New England Still Life,* exhib. cat. (Lincoln, Mass.: De Cordova and Dana Museum and Park, 1984), n.p.

11   JANE FREILICHER   *The Lute Player,* 1993

In this painting, as in *Bread and Bricks* (cat. no. 8), Freilicher combines a view into the landscape with an interior still-life composition. In this instance, however, she engages not only the dialogue between reality and artifice that is implied in the relationship between the tangible world of the spectator and the representational world of the painting but also the tension between different realms within the painting itself. Thus, the vase of flowers in the blue-striped vase on the bureau is juxtaposed with a watercolor by Freilicher of flowers in a glass vase. Then, in a stroke of metaphysical transposition, the guitar player from Jean-Antoine Watteau's painting *Mezzetin* (ca. 1718–20, Metropolitan Museum of Art) is seen both in a reproduction of the painting which sits stop the bureau and in "real" form in the garden outside.

This subtle demonstration of the duplicity of art and representation is reminiscent of the pictorial investigations of the Belgian surrealist René Magritte. Freilicher reinforces the notion of the window as a physical barrier (or entry) to a "third dimension" by emphasizing the reflective quality of the glass. The window frame, shades, and pull chords are all indicated by a shadowy reflected presence that seems to emanate from some space outside the painting.

Freilicher's painting *Bread and Bricks* depicts her studio in Manhattan, but here the view beyond the window shows the flat shoreline of eastern Long Island. The composition exploits the surprising transition from the lush eighteenth-century parkscape appropriated from the Watteau painting to the pale beaches of the Long Island Sound near Water Mill. Freilicher even designed her studio so that she could enjoy this specific view (which can also be seen in her *Autumnal Landscape,* of 1976–77, acquired by the Metropolitan Museum in 1978). Unfortunately, in the early 1980s, that landscape was bulldozed over, destroying a scene that had stimulated Freilicher's artistic vision for two decades.[1]

A postscript on the Watteau painting: Mezzetin was a stock character in the improvisational Italian theater known as the commedia dell'arte. He was frequently in pursuit of love that was not reciprocated. In Watteau's painting, he is shown singing a song in a vain attempt to win a lady. Freilicher has cropped the original scene, in which a marble statue of a woman, her back to Mezzetin, can be seen amid the trees over his right shoulder. This is an allusion to the unyielding object of Mezzetin's affection, who turns a deaf ear to his romantic song. Although Freilicher has titled her painting *The Lute Player,* the instrument that Mezzetin plays here, and in the Watteau painting, is actually a relative of the modern-day guitar.[2]   L S S

1 Margaret Mathews, "Jane Freilicher," *American Artist* (March 1983): 37.
2 I would like to thank my colleagues at the Metropolitan Museum of Art, William S. Lieberman, Jacques and Natasha Gelman Chairman of 20th Century Art; Katharine Baetjer, Curator, European Paintings; and Laurence Libin, Curator, Musical Instruments, for information on this painting, the Watteau, and the identity of the musical instrument in the painting.

HARVESTS, HUNTS, AND BOUNTIFUL SETTINGS

Harvest and hunt have been stock themes throughout the history of still-life painting. Age-old superstitions about insuring sustenance through visual symbolization may have provided an underlying motive for artists and patrons as still-life painting proliferated in Europe during the sixteenth century. The bountiful compositions of those earlier times are recalled in such modern examples as George Grosz's *Still Life with Walnuts* (cat. no. 14), Maud Cabot Morgan's *September Still Life* (cat. no. 15), and Jeanne Duval's *Still Life with Partridge and Corn* (cat. no. 18). Grosz's composition—a surprisingly domestic work from an artist known for his caustic political art satires—includes both the "raw material" of food cultivation (wheat, fruits, and nuts) and the "refined" produce (wine). Maud Cabot Morgan offers a variation on traditional hunting still lifes with her slightly more delicate display of

a dead hare and guinea hen, along with spice racks that indicate their preparation for consumption. The sturdy realism of Duval's work reflects her admiration for seventeenth-century Spanish and Italian painting while her peculiar combination of elements transcends time and place.

Since the Renaissance, still-life painters have been fascinated by feats of mimetic likeness and have attempted "to observe and record . . . velvet, fur, reflective metal surfaces, and the like."[1] It makes sense, then, that still life has been a perfect vehicle for the modernist deconstruction of academic painting through such tactics as minimizing illusionistic effects and reducing form to its bare essence. These specific tactics can be observed in the three other paintings in this section. Together, they demonstrate how an interest in painterly issues (as much as in the task of depiction) has characterized art in Europe and the United States in this century. The awkward shapes, dark contours, and thickly impastoed surface of Marsden Hartley's *Banquet of Silence* (cat. no. 12) reflect his interest in folk art, a concern that is prevalent in modern art. Nell Blaine's sumptuous *Big Table with Pomegranates* (cat. no. 16) eschews a meticulous rendition of surface, focusing instead on the organization of bold areas of color and rectangular shapes into a cohesive visual statement. In *Raspberries and Goldfish* (cat. no. 17), on the other hand, Janet Fish effects an unexpected distortion of what seems to be real. She captures our attention by establishing a spectacular, prismatic fracturing of color and reveling in its transformative effects on form. LSS

1 Karyn Esielonis, *Still Life Painting in the Museum of Fine Arts, Boston* (Boston: Museum of Fine Arts, 1994), 49.

Hartley's peripatetic life led him to Bermuda at least two times in his life—in 1917 and 1935. The first excursion, with Charles Demuth, marked "the beginning of Hartley's separation from avant-garde issues," according to art historian Barbara Haskell.[1] As a result, the 1917 Bermuda trip yielded a number of floral still-life compositions. By the time of his second trip to Bermuda, in the summer of 1935, however, Hartley was more interested in the marine life around the island. He made frequent boating excursions with the owner of the house where he lodged, and these experiences were reflected in his continued interest in fish themes through the following spring.

When he left Bermuda in September 1935, Hartley visited Nova Scotia for about six weeks before returning to New York. In Nova Scotia he stayed with the Masons, a local family who lived on Eastern Points Island, just off shore from the town of Lunenberg. Hartley reacted immediately to the ambience of the Mason household, writing to a friend, "There is a touch of Christian martyrdom about life anyhow, for they endure such hardship and hate any show of cheap affectation. All this vital energy and force. I have never been so near the real thing before."[2] According to Haskell, Hartley's experience of the "simple dignity and direct faith" of the Mason family—which contrasted with the more complicated and calculated relationships he had known previously—inspired him and, "as he came increasingly to value these qualities, his art grew spiritually richer."[3]

The title of this painting and the straight-forward presentation of the fish suggest that Hartley intended more than just a direct observation of a meal at the Mason home. Instead, he evokes the symbolic association of fish with the act of eating in such biblical allegories as the miracle of Christ's multiplication of the loaves and fishes. The fish is also a coded symbol for Christianity itself, an emblem that stems from the early years of the faith, when it was subject to official persecution and its adherents had to meet in secret.

Although elaborate presentations of food are common in still-life paintings, Hartley's rendition of the main course at the Mason's is anything but sumptuous. The three pale fish are laid out side by side on a bed of green leaves. Reddish roses surround the ensemble, which floats mysteriously before a white background. Clearly, Hartley was not interested in reproducing the textures or specific qualities of the fish but in the arrangement of their arced forms against the circular rosebuds. By selecting such a simple yet touching tableau, Hartley suggests the craggy sustenance of the fishing communities of Nova Scotia and Maine, a subject that dominated his work for at least a decade (as seen in his *Lobster Fishermen* of 1942, also in the collection of the Metropolitan Museum).   LSS

1 Barbara Haskell, *Marsden Hartley,* exhib. cat. (New York: Whitney Museum of American Art, 1980), 55.
2 Ibid., p. 98. Letter from Marsden Hartley to Arnold Rönnebeck, November 8, 1936, Archives of American Art.
3 Ibid.

When Walt Kuhn chose to paint a still life of fruit, he did not select one or two pieces as did his colleagues Max Weber, Henry Lee McFee, and Luigi Lucioni (see cat. nos. 41–43). Rather, Kuhn picked a robust barrel full of red and green cooking apples, probably MacIntoshes, from Dorset, a small town near the artist's summer house in southern Vermont.

Kuhn was always unconventional, and his path towards becoming a painter was no different. He grew up on the waterfront in Brooklyn, the son of German immigrants who operated a hotel for seamen. At the age of nineteen, Kuhn ran a bicycle repair shop and took part in bicycle races. Later, in California, he drew cartoons for the San Francisco *Wasp*. After traveling to Europe at the turn of the century he studied painting at the Colarossi Academy in Paris and then at the Royal Academy in Munich.

Back in the United States, Kuhn and his friend Arthur B. Davies helped to organize the famous Armory Show of 1913, which brought modern European art to America. Kuhn also acted as an art advisor to wealthy collectors like John Quinn, Lillie Bliss, and William Averell and Marie Harriman. The tall, ruggedly handsome Kuhn even dabbled in show business, organizing amateur theatricals, musicals, and vaudeville acts.

In 1925, after a serious bout with stomach ulcers made him reassess his life, Kuhn began to concentrate on painting. At that time he found the subject for which he is best known today: pensive-looking clowns, performers, and actors. In his large and cluttered studio on East 18th Street, Kuhn designed and supervised the manufacture of gaudy, spangled, and epauletted costumes to be worn by the performers he painted. He always allowed his models—show people rather than professional models—to choose their own clothes from his collection.

Kuhn generally had someone else set up his still-life arrangements. As *Apples from Dorset, Vermont* demonstrates, these compositions were often rather straightforward. But what was unusual was that Kuhn liked to depict only one kind of fruit at a time, and those in bulk. This practice was perhaps meant to defy the fetishized still lifes in the manner of Cézanne, so often copied by his fellow painters. Kuhn's avalanche of apples evokes instead fecundity and plenitude.   S R

All the elements of this handsome still life—the apples, the walnuts, the antique chair, the bundles of straw, and the bottle of pale dry sherry—evoke a warm hearth or a crisp autumn day. But the choice of these rather homely still-life objects might seem surprising if one considers that this work was painted by George Grosz, a dadaist and one of Germany's most anarchic and satirical artists. Just ten years before, Grosz's biting and fiercely antiwar collages had prompted a blasphemy suit against him in Germany. One might well ask, what changed?

In 1932, Grosz emigrated to the United States, following an invitation to teach for eight months at the Art Students League in New York. In 1933, a few weeks before Hitler's rise to power, Grosz decided to settle permanently in this country with his wife and two sons. Since childhood Grosz had been enamored with America, a country he knew only from adventure stories. After he became an American citizen, he embraced the "American Way" with uncritical enthusiasm for over twenty-seven years. Unfortunately, Grosz's infatuation with his newly adopted country rendered him blind to its contradictions. He was unable to see—let alone depict—his new surroundings with the same fiercely critical and satirical approach he used in Germany between the wars. In fact, Grosz turned into a typical American suburbanite. Photographs of the artist posing with his family in front of a small, unpresuming house on Long Island depict the kind of middle-class idyll he would have mocked in his earlier work.

The award of a Guggenheim Fellowship in 1937 allowed Grosz to give up teaching and to devote himself full-time to painting. He focused on traditional genres: self-portraits, nudes, apocalyptic visions, and a series of still lifes. Grosz chose the objects in this still life, no doubt, for their variety of textures and, perhaps because of their ordinariness—they are the kind of staples one usually has around.   S R

Were it not for her interest in travel, Maud Cabot Morgan might well have embarked on a political career in the late 1920s. A staunch supporter of Alfred E. Smith, she was encouraged by fellow Democrats to run for Congress in 1927. But instead she opted to go to Paris, where she met her future husband, painter Patrick Morgan. Between 1927 and 1931, Morgan associated with the expatriate colony of Paris and traveled extensively to post-revolutionary Russia, India, China, and Japan. During this time, Patrick Morgan encouraged her to take up painting. After their marriage in 1931, the couple moved to Munich to study painting with Hans Hofmann, a noted German artist and teacher who later influenced a generation of American abstract expressionists. The Morgans subsequently moved to Canada, where they lived in Quebec for four years. They returned to the United States in 1936, settling in New York City.[1] There, Morgan continued to study with Hofmann, who had emigrated to the United States. In 1938, Morgan had her first solo exhibition at the Julien Levy Gallery. *September Still Life* was purchased by the Metropolitan Museum from that exhibition.

Morgan's composition follows a traditional still-life format established in sixteenth-century Northern European painting. The dramatic diagonal of the dead hare (distinguished from a rabbit by its leaner torso and longer ears and legs) and the crumbled guinea hen are familiar motifs from historical examples. The distinctly masculine cast that is typical of this subject matter has here been domesticated by the presence of the stepped rack and the old wall container with its quaint scalloped backboard. These details suggest that the game is being presented as part of a routine meal preparation rather than as trophies or as a display of marksmanship.

There is little evidence in this painting of Morgan's eventual engagement with abstraction in the late 1940s. However, it does show an emphasis on painterliness as well as on description. The highlights on the netting of the drawstring bag in the background, the diagonal of the hare's body, and the spotted markings of the guinea hen create a visual continuity that compresses the space of the composition. Morgan has also reduced the chromatic values of the painting to shades of beige and muted hues of gray, beige, and green. The more intense bands of terracotta on the right edge and at the bottom of the composition suggest a source of illumination emanating from outside the painting.

In 1940 Morgan and her husband moved to Andover, Massachusetts, where he taught at Phillips Academy and she taught at Abbot Academy. Their home became a gathering place for students to hear jazz and talk about art. One of those students was the young Frank Stella.   LSS

1 Biographical sketch of Maud Cabot Morgan, Artists Files, Museum of Modern Art Library, New York.

Blaine has stated that this still life was a result of her "continuing love affair with flowers in interiors."[1] The painting represents a dinner setting laid out on the English refectory table in the artist's home in Provincetown, Massachusetts. The composition is based on a visual interplay of rectangular forms: the table itself, the white runner with black stitchwork, the chocolate mocha cake, and the four blue placemats. Other miscellaneous squares and rectangles on the table and in the background continue this motif. A further visual dialogue is established by Blaine's use of color. The yellow-and-clear-plastic salt-and-pepper shaker at the lower right echoes the yellow square between the two furthest blue mats; the red design on the matchbook next to the shaker picks up the red from the candle in the middle of the table; and the two blue rectangles on the wall rhyme with the blue placemats on the table.

The rectangular motif and color coordination serve as visual foils to the main still-life elements: the rosy pomegranates in the center foreground, the plate of fruit just above them, and the two white oval shapes to their right. The scene is dominated by the two vases of flowers, which the artist has identified as dahlias. Blaine only hints at the surface qualities of the porcelain table setting and the glass and earthenware vases. But she is at least

as successful as Janet Fish (*Raspberries and Goldfish* [cat. no. 17]) in conveying the sumptuousness of the occasion. Despite the seeming deliberateness of the organization, the artist says that the painting was finished rather quickly. She began late one evening and worked continuously through the night, completing the painting the next day.[2]

Blaine's study with Hans Hofmann in New York during the early 1940s accounts for the formal rigor of her painting. Along with her contemporaries Fairfield Porter, Alex Katz, Jane Freilicher, Leland Bell, and Louisa Mattiasdottir, Blaine was in the vanguard of the reemergence of a figural style in American art in the 1950s. This movement married the spontaneity of gestural abstraction, the structural rigor of cubism, and the impressionist love of light and color.   LSS

1 Nell Blaine, Artist's Statement (n.d.), Object Record Sheet, Departmental Archives, 20th Century Art Department, Metropolitan Museum of Art.
2 Ibid.

Janet Fish's reputation as "one of America's best known contemporary still life painters"[1] tends to observe her artistic origins in abstract expressionism. Fish initially focused on landscape painting, and in the 1960s and 1970s began to explore rendering fruit, which she rendered in abstract style. Then, she began to paint fruit and, slightly later, glass containers (sometimes filled with liquids). These diverse artistic directions come together in *Raspberries and Goldfish*. In the upper part of the composition is a clear glass goldfish bowl on a large blue glass plate. Next to it, further forward in space are two arrangements of flowers in glass vases. In the blue vase on the right are nasturtiums and what appear to be echinacea; on the left, another bunch of nasturtiums in a greenish vase react to a breeze. Just below the vases is a stack of empty glass plates that reflect the dark green tablecloth and the greenish yellow of the dotted Swiss curtains. The focus of attention at the extreme lower right is a metal or highly glazed ceramic bowl that is filled with raspberries, on which we can see the first fuzz of decay. Light from the window has produced multiple reflections and refractions throughout the complex tableau.

The spectator might feel somewhat overwhelmed by the scale of these items, seen so close at hand, and the dazzling display of color and light. In fact, the carefully studied effects of light on glass and other reflective surfaces tend to blind the viewer to the artist's adroit manipulation of the pictorial elements to suit her compositional goals. Despite the sensation of dramatic space—the setting is viewed from above—the floral arrangements actually block the rear half of the scene with a screen of stems and blossoms. This division is reinforced by Fish's use of hues of the same intensity throughout the composition, eschewing more atmospheric spatial techniques.

The breakup of the objects into color areas—which results from the artist's close observation of multiple reflections of objects of different colors on each vase, plate, and bowl—creates a dramatic all-over patterning. Our eyes move through the composition from one color shape to the other. Finally, Fish subordinates certain realistic details to the color transitions in the composition—from the reds, blues, and purples on the right to the sunnier oranges, greens, and yellows on the left—and in the process creates a new variety of deep purple nasturtium.[2]   LSS

1 Linda Cathcart, *American Still Life, 1945–83,* exhib. cat. (Houston: Contemporary Art Museum, 1983), 124.
2 I am grateful to Ben Feiman, Assistant Manager, Buildings Department, Metropolitan Museum of Art, for help in identifying flowers in this composition.

The local undertaker supplied the dead partridge for this still life. The bird had been struck by a passing car and was lying by the side of the road, where it was found by the undertaker, who was also the town's taxidermist. Knowing that Duval painted still lifes, he thought she might have use for the bird—and she did. The partridge inspired three still lifes, of which this is one.[1] To viewers familiar with the rarefied objects pictured in Duval's works of the early to mid-1980s—Delftware, bibelots, precious frames, objects, and small sculptures—the rural character of this composition might come as a surprise. But Duval admits that it was the chance receipt of the partridge that determined the rustic mood of this image, which brings to mind a country kitchen still life.

The artist divides her time between a small town in Italy and an even tinier one in New Hampshire, where she occupies the upper floor of a large, old former textile mill that she is in the process of restoring. An avid collector, Duval scours the local antique shops for objects that appear in her still lifes. She prefers what she calls the "classlessness" of simple wares, and hopes to recreate the "elegance, which was formerly attached to the objects, by the construction of her compositions, with their contrasts of light to shade."[2]

Duval arranged the red onions—those furthest to the left seem to float in space—ears of corn, old metal pitchers for oil and milk, dead bird, and wooden spoon as a frieze, parallel to the edge of the red-clothed table. She then focused the direction of the light to create the dramatic left-to-right movement from shade towards light. Duval was using a halogen light, which explains the almost surreal rustic clarity of the forms in the foreground. The lighting also brings into strong relief the feathery and frayed edges of the ear of corn and the white napkin. The artist delights in such details, which she calls "calligraphic."

Duval strives for a timeless realism in her paintings, one that bespeaks her admiration for Spanish and Neapolitan painting of the seventeenth century, especially the works of Caravaggio. For this still life, Duval's painstaking realism required many sittings. But in between, she always stored the partridge in her refrigerator.   S R

1 Jeanne Duval, conversation with author, August 2, 1995.
2 Ibid.

FLOWER PAINTINGS

Flower still-life paintings have as their subject either cut flowers in a vase or flowers growing in a pot. The earliest known flower still life in Western painting was painted in Germany in the mid-sixteenth century. Of course, images of flowers existed before that date, such as the vases of lilies frequently included in paintings of the Annunciation, but they were always included in larger compositions as mere accessories.

Nearly seventy years separate the earliest flower painting in this chapter, Marsden Hartley's *White Flower* (cat. no. 19), from the latest, Warren Brandt's *Beckmann Catalogue* (cat. no. 25). As Lowery Sims points out, Hartley's *White Flower* coincided with the artist's stylistic transition from cubism to a more sturdy figurative manner. In this work the flower and the vase resemble the simple wooden folk-art objects that interested Hartley at that time. In other words, Hartley's concerns were more formal than botanical in nature. Warren Brandt, on the other hand, displays a botanist's precision in the rendering of the flowers and potted plants in *Beckmann Catalogue*. It seems unlikely that Brandt chose these plants for their rarity or beauty. The potted primroses, philodendron, asters, and chrysanthemums are simply common, if reliable, houseplants.

Much more exotic are the flowers in Paul Wonner's still life *"Dutch" Still Life with Orchids, Postcard View of Paris, and "Death of Marat"* (cat. no. 53). From an assortment of containers—a beer bottle, a wine bottle, a Campbell's tomato juice can, a wine carafe, and a blue-and-white Delft vase—rise single stalks of exquisite flowers: rare orchids, a pink camellia, a yellow freesia, and a bunch of narcissus.

The odd mélange of the vessels and their curious placement—at different levels on the floor, on crates, and on a high stool—lends this ensemble the character of a makeshift shrine. It is like those spontaneous commemorations, haphazardly assembled with strange cheap vessels, that mark the very spot on the sidewalk where some hapless person fell victim to accident or murder. This one might be devoted to the French revolutionary Jean-Paul Marat (1743–1793), who was stabbed to death in his Paris bathtub. A postcard of Jacques-Louis David's famous painting of Marat (1793, Louvre) is propped against the back wall.

In his flower still life *An American Painting —For Rose Paul* (cat. no. 23), Ed Baynard commemorates his dead Russian grand-mother. Baynard did not think of his grandmother when he painted this now-famous image, serialized in half a million posters, but added her name to the title after the picture was given to the Metropolitan Museum. Mark Tansey's dryly titled *Still Life* (cat. no. 24) plays on such art-historical chestnuts as "still life" and "illusion versus reality." Having perfectly copied her flower still life—the painted version sits completed on the easel—the amateur painter flings the bunch of daisies into a wastepaper basket. It seems strange that this efficient homemaker would waste a perfectly fresh bunch of flowers.   S R

Marsden Hartley returned to New York City from an extended sojourn in Europe in the winter of 1915, after the onset of World War I. He spent the next two years traveling between New York and Provincetown, Massachusetts (summer 1916); Bermuda (winter and spring 1916–17); and Maine (summer 1917). During this period he evolved from a more frankly cubist style to one characterized by the sturdy figuration seen in *White Flower*.[1] The stark frontality of this work and its "primitive" character—thick, opaque paint surfaces and dark, heavily outlined forms—have been attributed to Hartley's strong interest in European and American folk art during the summer of 1917. These characteristics were further developed during his 1918–19 stay in New Mexico (see Hartley's *The Virgin of Guadalupe* [cat. no. 56]).

In *White Flower*, Hartley draws on conventions of floral still lifes that have existed since the sixteenth century. In traditional still-life painting such a close-up view of a flower would provide the occasion for a loving, carefully observed rendition of a blossom, recording all the textural qualities and formal peculiarities that distinguish one species of blossom from another. Here, the identity of the species of flower is not the point, despite the prominent size of the blossom. Set against the dark blue background, on a mottled dark blue surface, in a terracotta vase, the white blossom, surrounded completely by green foliage, seems curiously disembodied. The focus is less on the flower than on the formal and visual relationships between different color areas.

The majority of Hartley's floral paintings from this period—both those done in Bermuda and those made later in New York—were executed on glass. Hartley returned to flowers as his subject matter three years later, in 1920, and he continued to paint still-life subjects intermittently throughout his career. But, seen in his *Banquet of Silence* (cat. no. 12), these still lifes became increasingly religious and symbolic in nature, capturing the feeling if not the iconographic specificity of *The Virgin of Guadalupe*.

This painting was donated to the Metropolitan Museum by the American artist Raphael Soyer. Hartley gave it as a gift to Soyer, who had painted Hartley's portrait sometime in the late 1930s.[2]   LSS

1 This discussion of Hartley's work has been informed by Barbara Haskell's *Marsden Hartley* (New York: Whitney Museum of American Art, 1980).
2 See Raphael Soyer, *Diary of an Artist* (Washington, D.C.: New Republic Books, 1977), 244–45.

Although born in Montana, Edward McKnight Kauffer made his reputation in England. Kauffer went to Europe in 1913 with the intention of working in Paris. His trip was sponsored by Joseph E. McKnight, whose name Kauffer assumed as a gesture of gratitude for his support.[1] In Paris Kauffer immersed himself in the modernist styles that he had first encountered at the Chicago installation of the famous Armory Show. Within a year, however, Kauffer left for England, where he settled and worked for the rest of his life.

In London, Kauffer soon established a reputation as a skilled poster artist and graphic designer. His work incorporated the stylistic sensibilities of English modernism, specifically vorticism, a permutation of cubism and futurism. He became associated with various avant-garde groups, including the London Group (for which he served as secretary), the Cumberland Market Group (which grew out of the London Group), and Group X, a short-lived association of British artists formed in 1920 in the wake of Vorticism. Kauffer's most intense involvement with English modernism was between 1916 and 1921. During these five years, he functioned as a designer and visual propagandist for the new art, providing exhibition posters and catalogue covers for the London Group and the Arts League of Service, a group founded in 1919 to foster a new era of modernism after World War I.

Sunflowers was executed at the end of this five-year period, during which Kauffer also exhibited frequently as a painter. The aggressively "mechanical" aspect of these sunflowers demonstrates how the influences of van Gogh (whom Kauffer especially admired) and the Munich School had been supplanted in Kauffer's work by that of vorticism. In fact, there is an earlier study of these sunflowers, painted in 1917 (Government Art Collection, London), in which the flowers and the vase are rendered in softer, more curvilinear strokes. As in this work, the flowers sit on a hexagonal table, but there they are framed by draperies. In addition, there is a partition wall to the right, from which is suspended a shelf with three pears. In this painting, Kauffer has pared down the composition, omitting the classical pretense of draperies and interior architecture. In this later work, there is also a greater synthesis of cubist and futurist spatial conventions, particularly in the passage from the white vase to the table. Remnants of the earlier sunflower composition survive in the slight indication of a corner just above the largest sunflower head and in the fragment of a partition wall detectable in the odd juxtaposition of vertical and arced elements at the lower right.   LSS

1 The information in this essay has been informed by Mark Haworth-Booth's *E. McKnight Kauffer: A Designer and His Public* (London: Gordon Fraser, 1979).

Now largely overlooked in the annals of art history, Franklin Watkins was a noted presence in the American art world of the 1930s and '40s. Between 1913 and 1918 he studied intermittently at the Pennsylvania Academy of the Fine Arts, where his teachers included Adolph Borie and Arthur B. Carles. Watkins won two scholarships from the Academy to travel in Europe in 1917 and 1918, but the need to support himself and service in the United States Navy during World War I delayed his departure until 1923. Watkins finally traveled to France, Spain and Italy, and found himself particularly attracted to Venetian art of the fifteenth and sixteenth centuries and to the work of El Greco.[1]

Upon his return to the United States, Watkins was again stymied by financial difficulties. It was not until 1931, at the age of thirty-seven, that he first received national attention when he won first prize in the Carnegie International. His work generated extensive criticism from both conservative and progressive art critics. As a result, Watkins retreated for a few years, reemerging with a one-man exhibition at the Rehn Galleries in 1934.[2] Over the next three decades, Watkins was in great demand as a portraitist, and also became known for his religious paintings. He was commissioned to design ballet sets and costumes for Lincoln Kirstein, then director of the American Ballet Company. He occasionally turned to still-life painting.

In *White Roses,* Watkins presents a rather prosaic view of a bouquet set in a pitcher with a fluted foot. Despite his relatively loose rendering of form, Watkins successfully conveys a sense of the unique identity of the textures of each element in the composition. Several drooping stems and the leaves and blossoms that have fallen onto the table indicate that the bouquet is past its prime. The translucency of the tablecloth, suggesting a fine Egyptian cotton or muslin, is conveyed by the darker tonalities of the table, that show through. Although critics have ascribed the mannerist rendering and color in Watkins's work to the influence of Giorgione, Tintoretto, and El Greco, the artist also noted his interest in the work of Cézanne, which he encountered firsthand in a small exhibition organized by Carles at the Pennsylvania Academy of the Fine Arts.[3]   L S S

1 Franklin Watkins, interview with Paul Cummings, August 18, 1971, Archives of American Art, New York.
2 See Andrew Carduff Ritchie, *Franklin C. Watkins,* exhib. cat. (New York: Museum of Modern Art, 1950); and Henry Clifford, *Franklin Watkins,* exhib. cat. (Philadelphia: Philadelphia Museum of Art, 1964).
3 Watkins, interview.

This still-life composition by Karl Knaths was awarded first prize and was exhibited in *American Painting Today*, a national competition organized by the Metropolitan Museum in 1950. Knaths lived and worked for over a half century in Provincetown, Massachusetts, eschewing the art scenes of Boston and New York, and never traveling outside the United States. He learned the basic tenets of cubism from his sister-in-law who had studied in Paris with Albert Gleizes, and from other artists in Provincetown. Art historian Paul Mocsanyi once noted, "People used to say that . . . [Knaths] was the fellow who brought Paris to Provincetown. The truth is that Knaths brought Provincetown into the Paris School."[1]

Knaths is best known for his depictions of the clam diggers and fishermen of Provincetown, which he rendered in the cryptic, space-distorting conventions of cubism. He also had a distinctive palette that ran toward pinks, purples, and greens, and belied his early attraction to impressionist painting. In addition to these "wharf and shore scenes," Knaths painted "salty still life" compositions.[2] The exuberant *Basket Bouquet* is typical of his approach to form and color. The bright color of the lavender "cones" suggests that they are bunches of lilacs. The artist confirmed this identification in a review of the 1950 Metropolitan Museum exhibition, explaining, "There are a lot of old lilac bushes on this place, a hundred years old or more, so that over the years I've painted them many times in different pictorial procedures."[3]

The yellow form of the basket contains the lilac stems and the perky green leaves that spike up from the ensemble at intervals. The bouquet is set on a table that has a mottled, multicolored top and a bright orange apron underneath. Beyond the window at the back of the composition, Knaths has brushed in shades of yellow and brownish green to indicate foliage, and then articulated its branches with freely drawn squiggles. It is unclear whether the corner of a brown frame at the right is another element in the still life or simply a pictorial device added by Knaths to make us aware of the interplay of illusion and abstraction in this composition.   LSS

1 Paul Mocsanyi, *Karl Knaths,* exhib. cat. (Washington, D.C.: The Phillips Gallery, 1957), p. 11.
2 "Fair Competition," *Newsweek* (December 11, 1950): 20.
3 Ibid.

If this picture seems familiar, it is. It belongs to a series of some hundred still lifes—all depicting similar pots and vessels—that were so popular the artist created a best-selling poster of one of them. Nearly half a million copies sold, and the image was so ubiquitous in the late 1970s and early 1980s that even the artist grew "tired of seeing it, and hearing about myself everywhere. People kept knocking me off."[1] He retreated to the country to paint landscapes, quiet views seen through a window.

Still lifes remain Baynard's bread-and-butter subject, however. They come "naturally" to Baynard, a self-taught artist who first picked up a brush at the age of ten. After spending the decade of the 1960s in Europe, mainly Spain, France, and England, where he painted and did some commercial graphic work, Baynard settled permanently in New York in 1970.

All the works in Baynard's still-life series share the pale, monochrome background traversed by a thick horizontal line that serves as a ledge for an infinite variety of simple pots and vases. These vessels, seen only in silhouette and frontally, evoke birds sitting on telegraph wires. Their stark simplicity is offset by the rare flowers they often contain, either irises or orchids. In this work, the real iris on the right is echoed in the patterning of the vase on the left. While the bowls and vases are rendered as two-dimensional and frontal, a hint of modeling and perspective is visible in the flowers themselves.

Baynard sees himself in the tradition of the precisionists, heir to such American modernist painters as Charles Demuth and Georgia O'Keeffe. However, unlike the extreme close-up views of blossoms often rendered in O'Keeffe's paintings and some work by Demuth, Baynard keeps his flowers at bay. This distance and the overall emptiness of his compositions relate them to minimalism, a comparison the artist favors. As to why he titled this work *American Painting* given its Eastern sparseness and Zen stillness, the artist observes, "It's not fussy, it's quiet, it's very plain."[2] He considers plainness to be what is best in the American tradition, evoking wholesomeness and simplicity, qualities that he admires in Shaker furniture. When the painting was given to the Metropolitan Museum in 1980, the artist added to the dedication "For Rose Paul," to honor his late Russian grandmother.   S R

1 Ed Baynard, conversation with author, August 8, 1995.
2 Ibid.

Mark Tansey takes delight in teasing his viewers. In his large monochrome paintings he stages scenes in which he pokes fun at historical, art-historical, or literary expressions, clichés, or one-liners. Of course, he presumes an audience well-versed in these different fields to respond to the subtle visual puns that he presents in these tableaux. As so often in the artist's oeuvre, *Still Life* is a painting about a painting, and its tease is manifold.

The art-historical term "still life" generally applies to a painting of inanimate objects. In Tansey's work, the objects depicted in the still life resting on the easel are, indeed, "inanimate." But the flowers that served as the model for this still life are flying through the air—into the trash can. Such tongue-in-cheek allusions to art-historical chestnuts like "illusion" and "reality" abound in Tansey's work. His philosophical investigation of the different levels of meaning provoked by rethinking representation stems in part from his keen interest in semiotics, deconstructivism, and postmodernist theory.

From his enormous archive of found images, collected from sources as diverse as *Popular Mechanics* and art-historical monographs on Michelangelo, Tansey draws the images that serve as the "stock motifs" of his paintings. For a given project, he may scrutinize hundreds of pictures until he is content. He may also borrow poses or gestures from different figures and combine them in the final work. Tansey accentuates the dated quality of his source illustrations by limiting his palette to monochromes. His protagonists also frequently wear fashions from the 1940s. The female painter in *Still Life*, for example, sports the A-line dress, dainty apron, and high-heel pumps that became the virtual uniform of a generation of efficient homemakers in the early 1950s. In fact, Tansey culled this figure from a feature in *Popular Mechanics* that demonstrated how easy it was to use a new kitchen appliance.[1] Found titles are also important in Tansey, feeding into or playing off his visual puns. Typically, in *Still Life*, the supposedly inanimate object moves, the painter stands stock-still, and the still life is not a still life. S R

1 Mark Tansey, conversation with author, August 17, 1995.

"All my life I've been in love with Matisse,"[1] Warren Brandt once admitted. Indeed, his still lifes and interiors clearly demonstrate an admiration for the French master in their concentration on brilliant colors, varied textures, and decorative objects. However, they remain distinctly American in their faithful attention to fact. Brandt's truthful rendition of rather ordinary potted houseplants makes this still life unlike anything Matisse ever painted.

When Matisse depicted flowers—other than his favorite wild anemones—he usually generalized them into either colorful dots and petals or exotic green spiky leaves on long sinuous stems. Quite differently, Brandt brings a botanist's precision to the task of showing the differences between five plants: yellow, blue, and white field flowers; red primroses; burgundy philoden-drons; yellow chrysanthemums; and blue asters. The plants are lined up on a table in decorative pots that the artist's wife Clare bought in local antique shops.

Curiously, the objects in the foreground seem to belong to a different scale. The two small blue bowls of fruit and the match-book size Beckmann catalogue make the potted plants look gigantic. In fact, the catalogue, produced for the Max Beckman retrospective of 1994–95, is a hefty oversize volume of nearly five hundred pages. On the cover of the catalogue is a detail from Beckmann's life-size *Double-Portrait, Max Beckmann and Quappi* (1941, Stedelijk Museum), a work the artist painted during his wartime exile in Amsterdam.

Brandt had admired Beckmann's work since he had seen an exhibition of his work, at the Curt Valentin Gallery in New York in the early 1940s. So, later, when Brandt was studying painting at Washington University in St. Louis under Philip Guston, and Guston won a Guggenheim, Brandt suggested Beckmann as his temporary replacement. Although Brandt's own work reflects little of the German expressionist's style, as his student, he absorbed Beckmann's belief that rhythm and order must determine the overall structure of a composition. It was no doubt this concern for proper balance that determined the unusual yet harmonious scale of objects in Brandt's homage to the German master.   S R

1 *News from Hudson Hills Press*, press release for *Warren Brandt* by Nicholas Fox Weber, 1988.

INTERIORS AND GENRE SCENES

Artists' studios appear least affected by the changing tastes of interior design. The easel, worktable, bed, and other objects depicted some eighty years ago by Stuart Davis in his *Studio Interior* (cat. no. 26) would satisfy any self-respecting painter today. But who would want to live in the nondescript suburban *Interior* (cat. no. 27) painted by Preston Dickinson some seven years later? The paintings of interiors presented in this chapter cover a broad spectrum. With the exception of the Parisian antique shop shown in John Koch's *The Antiquarian* (cat. no. 30) and the Parisian studio depicted in Reginald Pollack's *Interior* (cat. no. 33), all of the works represent American settings. Some are invented, such as Randy Dudley's laboratory in *Verifying Dissonant Statistics* (cat. no. 36), and others, such as *The Victorian Parlor II* (cat. no. 28) by the African American painter Horace Pippin, just seem unreal. The naive charm and strict symmetry of Pippin's painting make it appear like a dollhouse or a stage set.

Asymmetry, instead, dominates Dickinson's *Interior*. The visually clashing but color-coordinated carpets, curtains, and upholstery reflect a certain misdirected modernist taste of the 1920s. Dickinson further emphasizes the claustrophobia the room induces by accentuating the closeness of the neighboring houses seen through the window. But a room need not be cluttered or claustrophobic to qualify as an interior. In Loren MacIver's interior titled *Hearth* (cat. no. 32), for example, we see only the tiny fireplace that occupies the far end of her skylit Greenwich Village studio. The remainder of the canvas is given over to the textured wall around the blazing fire. Although this interior has no furniture or figures, the cozy fireplace implies a human presence.

Although this exhibition is devoted mainly to still lifes and a few relatively uninhabited interiors, when figures are present in these paintings they are generally motionless. In John Koch's *The Antiquarian* (cat. no. 30), the artist's wife sits like an object among the antiquities in Ascher's shop on the rue des Beaux-Arts in Paris. Dora Koch literally blends into the furniture, as does two-year old Lizzie Porter at the far end of the breakfast table in her father's painting *Lizzie at the Table* (cat. no. 34). Fairfield Porter tried to emulate the dining room interiors of Pierre Bonnard, but he was forced to illuminate them with the unique harsh light of the New England coast.

Artificial light illuminates the two very different interiors by Randall Deihl and Randy Dudley, works that share an attention to a precise and lovingly detailed realistic style. Deihl's *Sweets* (cat. no. 35) depicts the actual lobby of a movie house in Northampton, while Dudley's *Verifying Dissonant Statistics* shows an imaginary scientist's laboratory. The protagonist in Dudley's picture is a young scientist who peers through a microscope at a gigantic wooden fish. Accessible only through high-security metal doors, the laboratory seems a rather forbidding environment. Glass jars containing colorful fish line the shelves behind the young scientist and have the playful air of those found in candy shops. By contrast, Deihl represents an actual candy shop and a real-life candy man, who stands behind the counter looking slightly sinister. The word "Sweets" appears somewhat incongruous above the balding, gnomelike figure with his pinky ring and intense stare.

Even more unconventional still-life objects, such as a manual typewriter and a steam iron, appear in Dona Nelson's *Daily News* (cat. no. 37). While artists of the German Neue Sachlichkeit (New Objectivity) movement in the 1920s tried to celebrate modernism by painting up-to-date furniture, telephones, and typewriters, Nelson has included a manual typewriter that even by the early 1980s was already obsolete. It was probably with a sense of irony, then, that Nelson chose to feature this quaint anachronism in a high-speed, computerized world.   S R

The opening of the Armory Show in New York City in 1912 was a catalytic event for the American art scene. It exposed American artists to a panoply of European modernist styles from expressionism to fauvism, cubism, and futurism. Although he was just nineteen years old, Stuart Davis exhibited three watercolors in this groundbreaking international exhibition, and the effects of the show itself were immediately evident in his work. Over the next few years he exchanged the social realism of the Ashcan School for a succession of skillful adaptations of European modernist styles. Ultimately, he developed into one of the most influential American modernist artists of this century.

This painting, an interior view of what was then the artist's studio, located in the Lincoln Arcade at 1931 Broadway in New York, seems to be a rehearsal for his future works. The center of the . composition is dominated by a view of New York City rooftops out the window, painted in cool blues and grays that contrast with the warm yellow and orange tonalities of the interior. In the absence of figures, the individual objects—bed, chairs, tables, books, glasses, bottles, paintings, a typewriter, a phonograph and an easel— assume the roles of dramatis personae in this composition. And Davis's subtle gestural affectations heighten the seeming

mutability and mobility of the lifeless forms. Soutine-like in its energy, Davis's squiggly brushstroke imbues the objects with an anthropomorphic character that parallels the sensibility of his slightly older contemporary Charles Burchfield.

The palette of this painting suggests more than a passing familiarity with Henri Matisse's 1911 composition *The Red Studio* (Museum of Modern Art, New York), which includes a comparable assembly of miscellaneous furnishings and artworks.[1] Although the Matisse cultivates an allover flatness that is considerably more abstract than Davis's composition, in both works the still-life objects have an almost organic link to their setting. And just as Matisse punctuates his red interior with white canvases, Davis uses the blue view out the window, the maroon tonalities of the easel and the phonograph, and the dull green coverlet on the bed to focus our attention on various areas within *Studio Interior.*   L S S

1 See Karen Wilkin, *Stuart Davis* (New York: Abbeville Press, 1987), 61–62.

The "modernistic" color schemes and patterns of the rather ordinary furniture in this room betray the vain attempt at decorating this middle-class suburban house. In fact, Dickinson lived with his sister in just such a house in Valley Stream, Long Island, until 1925, when she moved to the West Coast. Since Dickinson painted *Interior* in that year, he might have intended it as a sort of farewell to an all-too-familiar setting.

Little is known of the artist's early years in New York. His father was an interior decorator who later became a sign painter. Young Dickenson studied at the Art Students League in New York from about 1906 to 1910, and then spent the years 1910 to 1914 in Paris. He apparently avoided English-speaking colleagues in Paris, but associated with Charles Demuth. The two studied the Old Masters in the Louvre. Dickinson's future style was shaped by his admiration for Japanese prints and the art of Cézanne. After his return to New York, Dickinson adopted a hard-edged form of cubism, and he was frequently grouped with the precisionists of the 1920s. With few exceptions, his paintings and drawings are still lifes and industrial or urban land-scapes, subjects he treated with varying degrees of abstraction. In his New York scenes, for instance, he focused on working-class subjects like tenements, factories, smokestacks, and bridges, but rendered them formally as flat, sharply cut abstractions.

In *Interior,* the artist's tools of trade, a sharpened pencil, ink pen, and ink pot with green blotter all jut into the picture on the lower edge. Afternoon light streams into the room, but the time of day is made ambiguous by the partially concealed standing clock. The geometric patterns of the rug, chair, and sofa correspond to nondescript contemporary taste. A large, cut-crystal vase holds long-lasting cattails and accents the matching blues of the various curtains and table-cloths. Neighboring houses peek through the window. Their proximity accentuates the sense of claustrophobia the artist has so painstakingly recreated in this rather uninspired domestic view.   SR

A self-taught artist who worked in West Chester, Pennsylvania, Horace Pippin was "discovered" by the art world in 1937. Over the next nine years he established a flourishing career, becoming one of the most widely recognized African American artists in the country, and one of a small group of outsider artists who enjoyed patronage from the artistic mainstream. Having sustained a shoulder injury in World War I, Pippin worked slowly and laboriously. Despite this fact, he produced about one hundred and forty works on canvas and wood panel, and numerous drawings between 1930 and 1946. Pippin's subject matter includes themes from history (especially his own experiences fighting in the 369th Infantry Regiment), portraits, and political and religious allegories. He also painted tender and acutely observed scenes of the everyday lives of black and white Americans in and around West Chester.

Pippin lavished special care on the still-life studies, mainly floral arrangements and domestic interiors, that form a significant part of his corpus. In this painting the stunning, oversized floral arrangement competes for attention with the furnishings in this comfortable, well-organized interior. Pippin arranged an easy chair, a piece of furniture, and a framed painting symmetrically on either side of the vase of flowers. Only the character of these furnishings (a side table and lamp on the left, a bookshelf on the right) and a slight difference in the placement of the chairs are different on the two sides. Closer examination of the vase reveals a profile bust set within a framed area. These kinds of vignettes on vessels are frequently encountered in Pippin's interior scenes, as are the paintings-within-a-painting on the wall.

The basket of needlework at the foot of the chair on the right seems to suggest the presence of Pippin's wife, Jennie Fetherstone Giles Wade. Her intricately wrought crochet work—seen here under the flower vase and on the backs and arms of the chair—appears frequently in her husband's compositions. Pippin pays particular attention to the distinctiveness of each doily's design, as he does to the character of each of the flowers in the vase. Both Pippin and his wife were dedicated gardeners and maintained gardens not only around their house but also in a separate plot in West Chester.[1] Pippin carries his fascination for flowers over into the decoration of the gas lamp and the delightful repeated pattern of red flowers and green tendrils on the area rug. In paintings such as this, Pippin recorded scenes of comfortable domesticity, much like that in which he and his family lived. LSS

1 For a discussion of Pippin's still-life compositions, see Lynda Roscoe Hartigan, "Landscapes, Portraits, and Still Lifes," in Judith E. Stein et al., *I Tell My Heart: The Art of Horace Pippin,* exhib. cat. (Philadelphia: Pennsylvania Academy of the Fine Arts, 1994), 82–123.

The painstaking rendering of form and the ever-present suggestion of allegorical intent evident in this composition demonstrate why critics have described Priscilla Warren Roberts as a "romantic realist." In her work she has consistently shown an ability to demonstrate the "significance of the mundane" and to "evoke faint echoes of a dimly remembered dream."[1] Her meticulous paintings draw on the conventions of American still-life painters of the mid-nineteenth century, who combined scientific investigation with more picturesque elements, such as the use of light to evoke different moods and an interest in anecdote and temporality.[2]

Roberts's title calls attention to the purse made of carpeting that rests on the trunk in mid-composition. The carpetbag was a common traveling accoutrement in the nineteenth century, but is now best remembered as a symbol of the outside agitators, or "carpetbaggers," who figured in the political and social turmoil in the American South during reconstruction. In Roberts's painting, the bag—a reddish scarf spilling from it—sits atop a battered and peeling trunk, next to an equally frayed green hatbox. Three dusty books lie on top of the hatbox; a newspaper protrudes from the top one. Coiled beside these objects is an old feather boa that trails luxuriously to the floor on both sides. To the right, an umbrella hangs uneasily off a curtained

shelf, and on the back wall, an antique clock with a peeling face sets the time at four minutes to three. An old poster on the wall announces an "agricultural horticultural" exposition that took place over three days in September 1885.

The draped form at the lower left has been identified by the artist as a mannequin that is "pinch hitting" for the female owner of these goods.[3] Roberts recalls that the hatbox, carpetbag, and feather boa were acquired in various antique shops. But the trunk is a family heirloom with an interesting history. Roberts notes:

It made the trip back across the Pacific in 1892 with my father when his missionary family [in China] sent him home—all by himself at thirteen to go to school—He used to love to tell of how when he reached San Francisco . . . he sat on the trunk with a long suffering customs inspector, while he tried as best he could to remember what was in it—the key being lost.[4]

Roberts lavished great care on the depiction of each object in this painting. But despite the impression of illusionistic precision, close inspection reveals that Roberts has built up the scene in a series of minuscule, fluid brushstrokes. This approach reflects Roberts's great admiration for the work of the seventeenth-century Dutch painter Johannes Vermeer. Roberts studied at the Art Students League and the National Academy of Design between 1937 and 1943, and was elected National Academician to the Academy in 1957. LSS

1 Jeremyn Davern, "Now Voyager: Priscilla Roberts Explores Reality," *Illuminator* (Spring 1981): 26.
2 Wolfgang Born, *Still Life Painting in America* (New York: Oxford University Press, 1947), 22–25.
3 Priscilla Warren Roberts, Artist's Statement (1994), Object Record Sheet, Departmental Archives, 20th Century Art Department, Metropolitan Museum of Art.
4 Ibid.

Dora, the artist's wife, sits motionless amid the antique figures in this Paris curio shop. According to the artist, this painting was inspired by a visit to Ascher, the antiquarian on the rue des Beaux-Arts, in the summer of 1953.[1] Daylight from the shop window on the left bathes the high-ceilinged room with an even, diffused light reminiscent of the paintings of Johannes Vermeer, an artist whom the self-taught Koch studied closely.

Born into a well-to-do family, Koch sailed to Paris in 1928 at the age of nineteen. In 1933 he returned to New York, where he settled permanently. With Dora, a musician, he occupied a large, fourteen-room apartment on Central Park West that he filled with precious furniture, antiquities, objets d'art, and paintings by minor Old Masters and his own artist friends. This apartment served as the setting for many of his portraits and interiors. In them, his wife, students, friends, and models move through a comfortable, self-contained world filled with music and art, tea and cocktail parties, summer houses and subscriptions to the *New Yorker*. Handymen and window washers provide occasional glimpses of the outside world.

This small picture is exceptional in that it is not a showcase of the artist's social surroundings depicted in what some critics have derisively referred to as "illustrative realism." Here, the muted light adds a softness to all forms and lends a hushed stillness to this shop filled with antiquities from various centuries and cultures. Standing on the marquetry table in the foreground are a small marble figure and a bronze objet d'art. In the middle ground, the artist's wife is seated in a high-backed Spanish armchair, flanked with a large wooden African figure and a black basalt Egyptian cat. In the high glass case behind Dora are various Greek and Roman figurines and objects; others can be seen in the open cupboard on the left, which is topped by a standing Egyptian figure. Through the doorway in the back can be glimpsed a draped classical figure and what might be a Japanese screen in the darkened room. None of the objects depicted here appeared later in the artist's New York pictures. However, similar ones were part of the Christie's auction when the Koch estate was sold in 1989.   S R

1 John Koch, Artist's Statement, Object Record Sheet, Departmental archive, 20th Century Art Department, Metropolitan Museum of Art.

"I never intended to be a painter. I just liked to paint," MacIver confided to art historian John I. H. Baur in 1953.[1] MacIver began to paint, draw, and sketch in childhood. At age ten, she was allowed to attend the Saturday classes at the Art Students League in New York. MacIver wanted to draw models from life and that is what she did, wandering from class to class. However, the experience proved so exhausting for the ten-year-old that she left after one year. That was her only professional art training. In 1929, MacIver married the poet Lloyd Frankenberg, a high-school friend. They pitched their tent in Greenwich Village, where the widowed MacIver still lives today.

She joined the Pierre Matisse Gallery in New York in 1940 as that gallery's only American and only woman artist. In 1946 her work was included in *Fourteen Americans*, a landmark exhibition organized by Dorothy Miller at the Museum of Modern Art. In 1953 the couple traveled to Europe, staying mainly in Paris. During that trip, MacIver jotted in her small sketchbook ideas for later paintings. *Hardware (Quincaillerie)* was inspired by the notation "hardware in Paris . . . the noise that hardware makes."[2]

Her painting is a collagelike jumble that includes brooms, dusters, a frying pan, and a large blue pitcher, along with assorted samples of linoleum and wallpaper. MacIver also points out that she included nails, pliers, and screwdrivers, and topped it all by the letters "JAVEL 1 CROIX," which refer to the brand name of a French bleach. The artist liked the blue pitcher so much that she brought it back from Paris and included it in several other paintings. Filled with dark red cherry twigs, the pitcher stands today on a balustrade outside her studio. MacIver was also attracted to the speckled linoleum that can be seen at the far right of the composition. She brought back a roll of that also and used it to cover the floor of her husband's writing loft.

MacIver has a poet's sensibility. She sees beauty in banal, everyday objects, and makes them the subjects of her art. She once wrote, "My wish is to make something permanent out of the transitory."[3] Motifs as diverse as a studio skylight, a drop of rain or oil, a patch of broken asphalt with a child's hopscotch design, the lid of an ashcan, a battered window shade, and a rickety fireplace, have all been transformed into art by her poetic vision.

The tiny fireplace shown in *Hearth* is at the far end of the artist's skylit studio on Perry Street, in a house that once belonged to painter John Sloan. In this painting MacIver applied an uncharacteristically heavy impasto in an effort to imitate the marzipanlike texture of her studio walls. The picture shows MacIver's typical fascination with the contrast between the opaqueness of the textured gray stone wall and the iridescence of the flickering reddish flames, which seem to emanate from somewhere behind the canvas. Today, the artist hardly uses the fireplace. It draws too well for the tiny opening and the flames scorch the wall, just as shown in the painting.   S R

1 John I. H. Baur, *Loren MacIver/I. Rice Pereira*, exhib. cat. (New York: Whitney Museum of American Art, New York, 1953), 8.
2 For MacIver, the sound of the French word *quincaillerie*—the painting's original title—evokes the hard noise of metal hardware. MacIver, conversation with author, August 24, 1995.
3 Dorothy Miller, ed., *Fourteen Americans*, exhib. cat. (New York: Museum of Modern Art, 1946), 28.

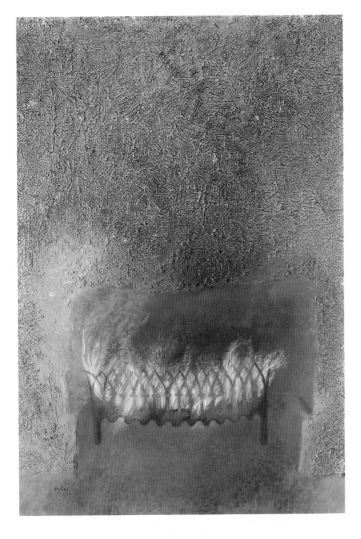

"I loved painting in blues in those days," remembered Reginald Pollack when asked about this mostly blue *Interior* from 1958.[1] The work was created during Pollack's twelve-year stay in Paris, from 1948 until 1959. It was only after he got to Paris that he decided to become an artist. He had worked as a studio apprentice for the painter Moses Soyer before World War II, and after the war he kept afloat as a freelance window designer for New York department stores. But in 1948, with support from the G.I. Bill, he settled in Paris to teach himself to paint. There, he encountered the greatest influence on his life as an artist, the sculptor Constantin Brancusi.

Pollack first visited the famous master at his studio at 11 Impasse Ronsin in 1948. He left awed, as well as eager to find his own studio at the Impasse, a collection of five rows of artist's studios in Montparnasse built around the turn of the century. With the exception of Brancusi's large studio, the others were simple rooms with high, skylighted ceilings, but no kitchens, bedrooms, or bathrooms—just a sink with a cold-water tap.[2] In the early 1950s, the studio right next to Brancusi's became empty, and Pollack moved in. It was a ruin; the ceiling had half fallen in and the rotting walls had been painted clay-pot red by its former occupant, the painter Odilon Redon. It took Pollack three months to restore the room and paint it white. "Brancusi was the patriarch of the Impasse," Pollack recalled.

"He inspired instant respect."[3] In fact, Pollack regarded himself as an apprentice to Brancusi, who was then in his late seventies. He often visited the old artist, helping him with odd jobs around the house. From time to time, Brancusi, who himself never accepted invitations, would ask Pollack and his wife over for champagne and biscuits.

Interior is one of a series of works that celebrates the light-suffused studio at the Impasse, in which Pollack spent his formative years. Whereas the walls are almost empty—except for two tacked-up pictures—the room is cluttered with stools and chairs, objects that the artist still collects. The loosely brushed composition represents his awkward, yet luminous attempt to construct space through strokes of color. He was attempting to apply the lessons he had learned by looking at the interiors of Pierre Bonnard and Henri Matisse.   S R

1 Reginald Pollack, conversation with author, August 28, 1995.
2 This information on the Impasse Ronsin is taken from an article by Pollack about living next door to Brancusi. See Reginald Pollack, "Shaman and Showman," *Art & Antiques* (May 1988): 94 ff.
3 Pollack, conversation with author.

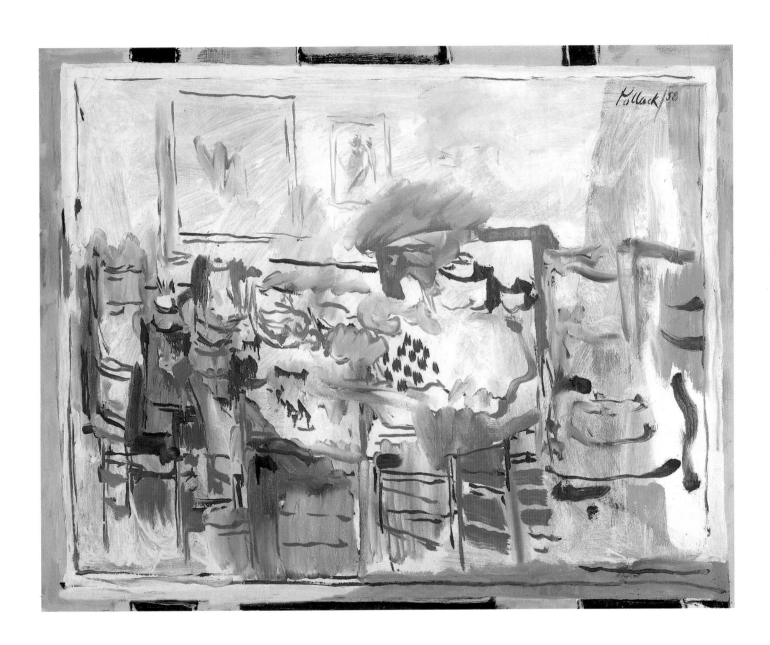

Like his heroes Bonnard and Vuillard, the New England "intimiste" Fairfield Porter focused on his own surroundings. Porter's wife, poet Anne Chaning Porter, his five children, and his friends make numerous appearances in his paintings. The small child sitting in a highchair at the end of the breakfast table in this painting is the artist's two-year-old daughter Elizabeth, known as Lizzie. Porter also liked to depict life in the airy houses where he and his family lived: the rambling captain's house in Southampton on Long Island and the smaller summer cottage on Great Spruce Head Island in Maine. Both a prominent painter and a writer on art, Porter counted among his friends painters Elaine de Kooning, Larry Rivers, Jane Freilicher, and Jane Wilson, and poets John Ashbery, Frank O'Hara, James Schuyler, and Kenneth Koch.

With regard to the objects in his works, Porter explained, "In still lifes, I don't arrange them . . . usually it is just the way the dishes are on the table at the end of a meal—it strikes me suddenly. And so I paint it."[1] Indeed, the various dishes casually arrayed on this breakfast table suggest one of those pleasant summer meals that stretches on and on. The objects include a hodge-podge of the elegant and the practical: the blue-and-white Delft plate, the gold-and-white porcelain cup and saucer, a decorated English plate, a celadon green bowl, a white enamel coffee pot, a little English ceramic sugar bowl and a jar of English orange marmalade. As a personal note, the artist has included a volume of poetry by Wallace Stevens, his favorite poet. The reddish foliage from a copper beech mixed among the bunch of flowers—lilies and field flowers—adds a darker shade to the light-filled interior.

After graduating from Harvard in 1928, Porter studied at the Art Students League in New York with Boardman Robinson and Thomas Hart Benton. Later he traveled in Europe, spent time in Italy, and settled in New York, before moving to Southampton in 1949. He associated with the writers of the *Partisan Review,* and through his friendship with Elaine de Kooning he later became an art critic for *Art News* and wrote for *The Nation*, *Art in America*, and *Evergreen Review*. After he gave up writing on art in the mid-1950s, he concentrated fully on painting and produced his best works.   S R

1 Paul Cummings, "Interview with Fairfield Porter," *Archives of American Art Journal* 12, no. 2 (1972): 10–21.

Randall Deihl is a chronicler of what he calls "kitschy America," the rapidly disappearing diners, theaters, and storefronts of the small towns. In the places so full of memories, Deihl presents his own "little 'dramas' of mystery, ambiguity, and alienation."[1] *Sweets* presents a ready-made "drama" the artist found in the lobby of his local movie house, the former Academy of Music, in Northampton, Massachusetts. Tucked between the Beaux-Arts architectural elements of the worn foyer, Deihl discovered a gleaming shack counter manned by a sinister-looking proprietor. The blithe mingling of old and new is encapsuled in the plastic "stained-glass" Coca-Cola lamp that hangs between the two period Tiffany stained-glass overdoors.

Deihl had visited this place for years before commemorating it in *Sweets.* The Academy of Music, on Northampton's Main Street, was built in 1891 in a Beaux-Arts style. It was the first municipal theater in the United States, and hosted concerts, operas, and dramas. In 1912 the building housed a theatrical stock company that presented different plays each week with such well-known members as William Powell and Jane Rennie. In 1950 the Academy was reopened as a movie theater playing classical films, and once again it became the cultural center of this small college town.

The painting is based on careful drawings done on site—highly detailed and finely delineated studies of the soft-drink cooler, the popcorn machine, and the shiny trash can. The artist took poetic license with just a few telling readjustments. For instance, he heightened the light intensity of the reflections cast by the counter and the popcorn machine. Also, instead of the bushes actually seen through the window in the exit door on the left, Deihl depicted a church and road signs.[2] Finally, he added a cheap reproduction of Edward Hopper's famous painting *New York Movies* (1939, Museum of Modern Art) to match the forlorn mood of the counterman, Tommy Bruno. A local character, Bruno was in his fifties when Deihl painted him. Bruno visited the artist's studio regularly for about a month to pose for his portrait. As a result, Deihl was able to capture Bruno with clinical precision: his dwarf-like stature, his huge balding head, his pudgy arms and hands, and his distinctive pinky ring and digital watch. Judging by his immaculately clean counter, Bruno ran a tight ship. Some of his regimentally arranged candy boxes show up as tiny reflections in his squarish horn-rimmed glasses. After the painting was first exhibited in Northampton, Bruno, who saw nothing odd in his portrayal, became a town star. Sadly, he died of a heart attack in 1993.   S R

1 Randall Deihl, Artist's Statement, (April 18, 1988), Object Record Sheet, Departmental Archive, 20th Century Art Department, Metropolitan Museum of Art.
2 Randall Deihl, conversation with author, August 9, 1995.

Verifying Dissonant Statistics is Randy Dudley's tongue-in-cheek portrayal of an earnest scientist at work. Seated at his laboratory table, the bespectacled researcher peers through his microscope at an unfamiliar-looking, red-striped, green fish. In the notebook on the table, the young scientist will record his findings. There are two large jars on the table, one preserves specimens of similar fish, the other has been opened. Stacked on shelves behind the scientist, several smaller bottles of disparate height hold different ichthyological specimens. The entrance to the room is fortified by an elaborate mechanical apparatus that can close to protect whatever dissonant statistics are being verified. The scientists research is clearly "classified."

In Dudley's painting, the setting is recorded so precisely that no camera is necessary. It seems to be a thoroughly objective—even scientific—rendition of the scene. The spectator, however, should be alert. We must be as inquisitive as the scientist portrayed. Did similar studies in equally guarded places produce an atom bomb? And why is this laboratory room, a place of such serious study, submerged in water? And will the water recede or rise?

It might be argued that the painting relates to studies in evolution. The scientist may be examining evidence relevant to the origins of life, in which case the flooded laboratory might allude to the primeval environment from which man struggled to stand. Also, water often stands for the subconscious, the irrational, the element in which all intellectual structures dissolve. Perhaps the painting is a cautionary tale: should the scientist become locked into his research, as he appears to be, he will drown. Is Dudley warning us of the dangers of focusing too much on the past? Is this small painting so profoundly anti-intellectual? While such speculations add dimensions to the painting's narrative, they may have nothing to do with the artist's intent. Perhaps he simply hopes that scientists themselves will laugh when they look at this picture.   WSL

This wry composition provides a perfect 1980s version of the traditional tabletop still life. It is the kitchen table of any number of urban households in America. Nelson has noted that all the details of this scene were observed from real life, right down to the rather disjointed headlines in the newspapers—one referring to nuclear buildup, the other to sports. An indolent and insouciant feline pet, demanding attention, has planted itself centerstage. The table's multiple functions are signaled by the teapot, the typewriter, the iron, and the hammer. Finally, the corporal presence created by the jacket that hangs over the chair in the foreground provides clear evidence that still-life elements can "be brought to bear on the portrayal of the human subject."[1]

Nelson has tilted up the perspective of the tabletop so that we have a clear view of the accoutrements of her life. In fact, the spatial anomaly is so exaggerated that the entire table seems ready to sail out the yawning aperture of the lunetted window. The sense of controlled chaos in interior space is amplified by Nelson's crowding of the oversized chairs around the table. In addition, there is a misalignment of the folk pottery and the saw attached to the far wall. As if this were not enough, the artist's almost obsessive rendering of the wood grain of the table further unsettles the scene and threatens to steal all the visual attention. By contrast, the blue moonlit sky visible out the window is thoroughly placid and calming. The symmetry of the two towers of the building across the way reinforces this feeling. Nelson herself has alluded to the jarring contrasts in this scene. "I was struck by the moon's cold eternal gaze in relation to the self-destructive activities of human beings . . . and the passing sports scores," she notes. "One day I fully expect to see 'World Ends' presented right along with 'Yanks Down 2.'"[2] LSS

1 Cornelia Lauf, ed., *Natura Naturata (An Argument for Still Life),* exhib. cat. (New York: Josh Baer Gallery, 1989), n.p.
2 Dona Nelson, Artist's Statement (n.d.), Object Record Sheet, Departmental Archives, 20th Century Art Department, Metropolitan Museum of Art.

Book of Hours: Winter is composed of two separate panels. The door and the burning candle depicted on these panels have the stark simplicity of images found in grade-school primers. This still life is part of a series of ten to twelve works that Ott titled "The Book of Hours"; all are either diptychs or triptychs. The artist borrowed the title *Book of Hours* from the small prayer books of the late Middle Ages that were notable for their sumptuous illuminations.

How do a candle and a door allude to winter? Ott explains that a door offers protection against the cold, while a candle supplies light during the dark winter months.[1] Still, the juxtaposition of the door and the burning candle remains somewhat puzzling. Also, the scale of the two objects is incongruous. By combining simple images in unexpected ways, Ott strives to elicit from her viewers a new meaning. Another aspect of the artist's work is its sheer "physicality." Ott used large housepainter's brushes to make these expressionistic brushstrokes, what she calls her "marks of a painter."[2] She stopped using these brushstrokes many years ago and now works in encaustic, which she says gives her the feeling of "carving her paintings."[3]

Born in New York City, Ott spent most of her life on the West Coast. She attended the San Francisco Art Institute, graduating with an M.F.A. in 1981. Since then, she has lived mostly in Los Angeles, while exhibiting in New York. In January 1996, Ott began teaching painting at Washington University in St. Louis. There, some fifty years earlier, one of Ott's heroes, Max Beckmann, also served as a painting instructor after fleeing his native Germany.   S R

1 Sabina Ott, conversation with author, September 7, 1995.
2 Ibid.
3 Ibid.

TABLE STILL LIFE

The tradition of the "table still life" has two great masters, Jean Siméon Chardin (1731–1768) and Paul Cézanne (1839–1906). The influence of these two French painters reverberates today in the works of some of the artists who are presented in this section. Chardin was the first artist to paint still lifes of commonplace objects, usually food and kitchen utensils. The artist who learned most from Chardin was Cézanne. As art historian Charles Sterling points out in his seminal study of the still life, it was only with Cézanne that still life ceased to be a sideline in the career of a great artist. Cézanne made still life equal to landscape and gave it precedence over portraiture.[1] Cézanne incorporated still-life setups in many of his larger compositions, often working from simple props he kept in his studio. These props have since become so famous that they are forever associated with him—Provençal pots, dark wine bottles, plaster casts, small faience sugar bowls, groups of apples or oranges, and crumpled napkins. Some of these elements, so familiar from Cézanne's works, were adopted by Henry Lee McFee for his *Still Life with Striped Curtain* (cat. no. 42) and by Max Weber in *The Celadon Vase* (cat. no. 43). Italian-born Luigi Lucioni also chose objects we now associate with Cézanne—a plain table topped by simple objects, fruits, and a crumpled napkin— for his *Pears with Pewter* (cat. no. 41). However, Lucioni's effect is very different. His highly polished style turns textures and colors into something more intense than what is possible in nature.

Joseph Hirsch's realistic *Melons* (cat. no. 50) and Raymond Saunders's far more abstract *Something About Something* (cat. no. 51) illustrate the range of styles employed in the table still life. Saunders mingles large abstract planes with outlines of still-life objects, stenciled numbers, and lettering, techniques that link him to the tradition of synthetic cubist collage. Much earlier, Stuart Davis also looked closely at the collages of Braque and Picasso when composing his 1924 still life *Edison Mazda* (cat. no. 40). In that painting, Davis skillfully balanced a portfolio, a goblet, and a lightbulb in the shallow space of the cubist collages. Likewise influenced by the cubists was A. E. Gallatin; however much he abstracted his forms in *Number 28 (Still Life)* (cat. no. 45), they still suggest a still life.

By breaking up, rather than reducing, his still-life objects, Yasuo Kuniyoshi introduced narration into his *Broken Objects* (cat. no. 47). Smashed bits and pieces culled from the artist's personal life express Kuniyoshi's bitter feelings at having been classified as an "enemy alien" after the bombing of Pearl Harbor in 1941. The broken crockery and china on Valerio's large, cluttered table in *Still Life with Decoy* (cat. no. 54) are displayed for less political though equally dramatic effects. Mirrors placed on and next to the table duplicate

the already complex and dramatically lit composition. With Valerio's still life, the tradition seems to have entered a new phase. From its early modesty in size and content, as initiated by Chardin, it has evolved, in the hands of artists like Valerio, into dramatic stage-setting.   S R

1 Charles Sterling, *Still Life Painting: From Antiquity to the Twentieth Century*, 2nd rev. ed. (New York: Harper & Row, Publishers, 1982), 128.

Samuel Halpert was among the first American artists to be influenced by modern art in Europe. When he first went to Paris in 1902 as a sixteen-year-old, his arrival preceded that of his American contemporaries by several years. However, unlike many of them, Halpert and his art are little known today.

Halpert was five years old when his family came to New York from Russia in 1889. Ten years later, after his talent was recognized and supported, he enrolled at the National Academy of Design. When he went to Paris in 1902, he studied at the Ecole des Beaux-Arts under Léon Bonnat. However, he soon rejected formal instruction, preferring to work independently with his French colleagues, among them Robert Delaunay and Albert Marquet. Open and responsive to the newest art he encountered in artist's studios and galleries in Paris, Halpert soon developed a style related to fauvism but with less high-keyed colors and more stable forms.

During his two-year-long return to New York from 1912 to 1914, Halpert played a key role in fostering the growth of modern art in the United States. In addition to acting as an agent for his Parisian colleagues Patrick Henry Bruce and Robert Delaunay at the Armory Show in 1913, Halpert exhibited two paintings of his own in that pioneering show. He returned to Europe in 1915 and traveled with Robert and Sonia Delaunay to London and Spain. While at Vil do Condo on the Atlantic coast of

Portugal during the summer of 1915, Halpert painted *The Red Tablecloth*. The white pitcher, reddish teapot, black knife, and various fruits seem casually arranged on the long, narrow table. While Halpert adopted the sort of objects featured in the classic still lifes of Cézanne, he was apparently less concerned with the architecture of form than was the Aix master. Instead, Halpert focused on the brilliant coloristic effect of the red, decorated country cloth that neatly covers the entire table.

When he returned to the United States permanently in 1916, Halpert continued to paint the themes he had developed in France—mainly still lifes and interiors but also plein air landscapes and cityscapes. In 1918, he married Edith Gregor Fein, who founded the Downtown Gallery in New York in 1926. After their marriage broke up in 1927, Edith Gregor Halpert went on to establish herself as one of the pioneer dealers of American modern art. In 1928, she organized an exhibition of her husband's work but did not promote his work after that date. Halpert headed the painting department at the school of the Society of Arts and Crafts (now the Center for Creative Studies) in Detroit until his untimely death in 1930, at the age of forty-six.   S R

This painting is one of several by Davis featuring a light bulb. This motif first appears in studies he made during a trip to New Mexico in the summer of 1923. Despite the seductions of the desert landscape, Davis apparently spent most of his time in Santa Fe, working in a room littered with saws, egg beaters, and light bulbs, and illuminated by a bare bulb hanging from the ceiling. His works from this time are painted in muted grayish-green, pale-blue, and gray tonalities, as if he were deliberately suppressing the vibrant natural environment around him. In several, the still-life elements become so large they overwhelm the landscape elements.

The first commercially viable incandescent light bulb was developed by the American inventor Thomas Alva Edison in 1879. The trademark "Mazda," mentioned in the title of this painting, was adopted by General Electric in 1909 to distinguish light bulbs that were manufactured according to certain prescribed standards for illumination. The word itself is an Iranian derivation of the Sanskrit word for science, and refers to the Zoroastrian god of law, justice, truth, and light. "Edison Mazda," therefore, identifies bulbs produced at the Edison Lamp Works in Harrison, New Jersey, which met the Mazda standard. *Edison Mazda* introduces the light bulb to a cubist still-life format, replacing the more conventional fruits, playing cards, pipes, and musical instruments. Here, Davis has arranged the light bulb, a glass, and a portfolio on a tabletop or a shelf, a compositional format he favored.

There are clear indications of Davis's deep appreciation of cubism in his representation of distinct flat, patterned planes. One can also detect the influence of the purist aesthetic of Fernand Léger in Davis's emphasis on pristine forms accentuated by dark outlines. The bold juxtaposition of a traditional still-life object—the cut-crystal glass—and an industrially produced light bulb signals a juncture not only in Davis's own work but also in twentieth-century American still-life painting.[1] In his other representations of the light bulb in this series, Davis painted it with the distinctive corrugated packaging that is still used today. These paintings, along with his earlier studies of cigarette packaging, indicate Davis's fascination for commercial advertising and graphic design, an interest he shared with painter Gerald Murphy. Four years after the light bulb paintings, Davis began a year-long study of a still-life composition of an eggbeater, a rubber glove, and a fan. Those works are generally considered to be the most important abstract paintings in American art at the time.   LSS

1 For a discussion of Davis's still-life compositions of the 1920s, see William Agee, *Stuart Davis (1892–1964): The Breakthrough Years, 1922–1924*, exhib. cat. (New York: Salander-O'Reilly Galleries, 1987), n.p.

41   LUIGI LUCIONI   *Pears with Pewter*, 1930

When *Pears with Pewter* entered the Metropolitan Museum's collection in 1932, Luigi Lucioni became the first contemporary American artist to have his work hung at the museum.[1] The son of an immigrant coppersmith from northern Italy, Luigi Lucioni was an American success story. He was only ten years old when his family came to the United States and settled in New Jersey. At the age of fifteen, he attended night classes at Cooper Union in New York City. Later he enrolled at the National Academy of Design, supporting himself as an illustrator for newspapers and magazines. In 1925 he completed his formal education and set off to visit the museums in Italy, where he fell under the spell of the Renaissance masters. Through luck, industry, and a winning personality, he had his first one-man exhibition at the Ferargil Gallery in New York in 1927.

Lucioni is best known for his landscapes of Vermont, where he spent the summer months, and for the still lifes he painted during the fall and winter months in New York. His immaculately realistic works were immediately successful, finding buyers and inspiring rave reviews. Art critic Henry McBride, writing in the *New York Sun*, described Lucioni as "the most popular painter that this country has produced since Gilbert Stuart."[2] It was Lucioni's Old Masterish still lifes like *Pears with Pewter*, a typical example of the artist's work at that time, that inspired such hyperbolic responses from critics in the 1930s. To today's viewer, this arrangement of a pewter pitcher, a water glass, a cloth napkin, and some apples and pears on a gleaming flip-top mahogany table inevitably appears extremely competent but thuddingly academic.   S R

1 The museum actually purchased another painting by Lucioni titled *Dahlias and Apples,* but when the curator saw *Pears with Pewter* and liked it better, an exchange was arranged. Stuart P. Embury, *The Etchings of Luigi Lucioni: A Catalogue Raisonné,* (Holdrege, Nebraska: Jacob North, Inc., 1984), 10.
2 Quoted in "Lucioni," *The Art Digest* (January 15, 1936): 11.

42   **HENRY LEE McFEE**   *Still Life with Striped Curtain,* 1931

In the 1930s Henry McFee was regarded as one of America's foremost artists. His paintings were exhibited, published, and acquired by major museums and collectors.[1] Yet, today his formalist realist work is barely known.

McFee was born in St. Louis in 1886. A modest inheritance allowed him to devote himself full time to painting. In 1908 he studied landscape under Birge Harrison at the summer classes of the Art Students League in Woodstock, New York, where he lived for the next twenty years. Later he moved to San Antonio, and in 1942 he became a professor in the graduate school of Claremont College in California, where he lived until his death in 1953.

McFee belonged to the generation of American artists that looked for inspiration to the established modernist artists of the School of Paris, notably Cézanne, Picasso, and Braque. McFee never traveled to Europe but received information about European art from his friend, painter Andrew Dasburg.

McFee's painterly yet somewhat uninspired style is demonstrated in *Still Life with Striped Curtain,* which depicts a corner of the artist's studio. The Cézannesque country table is framed like a small stage set by the striped curtain on the left and a gray wall on the right. Various fruits lie casually strewn before the high-stemmed bowl, the brush holder, and book, as if they had casually tumbled from the crumpled brown-paper wrapping. Everything about this work—the muted colors, the space, the angle of inclination from above, and the choice of timeless objects—evokes the still lifes of Cézanne. But after a brief flirtation with this Cézannesque style, McFee retreated to a more realistic mode.   S R

1 John Baker, *Henry Lee McFee and Formalist Realism in American Still Life, 1923–36* (London and Toronto: Associated University Presses, 1987), 86.

4 3   MAX WEBER   *The Celadon Vase*, ca. 1933

Today Max Weber is most acclaimed for his cubist-futurist depictions of New York City of the mid-1910s. He captured the city's cacophony and discord in such now-famous pictures as *Rush Hour, New York*, *New York at Night*, and *Grand Central Terminal*, all painted in 1915. These works have been called "the most successful early abstractions produced in this country."[1]

The son of a Russian tailor, Weber emigrated to New York in 1891 with his parents. The family settled in Brooklyn. From 1898 to 1900 Weber was enrolled in art classes at Pratt Institute, where he studied design with Arthur Wesley Dow. Living in Paris between 1905 and 1908, Weber came to know most of the advanced artists, including Picasso and the fauvists. He also became a close friend of Henri Rousseau. In 1908, Weber attended an art class taught by Matisse.

Weber returned to New York in 1909 steeped in the European aesthetic. American critics reacted negatively to the fauvist, cubist, and futurist tendencies in his work. However, he had a few staunch supporters, including photographer Alfred Stieglitz and English art critic Roger Fry. Stieglitz gave him a one-man exhibition at his gallery 291 in 1911, and Fry invited him to exhibit with the Grafton Group in London in 1913.

In the 1920s, Weber followed the general trend toward representational art, a tendency shown in his understated still life *The Celadon Vase*. Celadon is a kind of pottery, originally produced in China, that has a distinctive pale grayish-green glaze. The shape of this particular vase identifies it as a modern Western product. In general, this still life is characteristic of the artist's oeuvre in the 1930s. Excepting the composition's overall sense of symmetry and order, *The Celadon Vase* shows that Weber never forsook the lessons of Cézanne. The plain background, the simple wooden furniture, and the bottle, vase, napkin, and fruits casually strewn over the tabletop all derive from the Master of Aix.   S R

1 John I. H. Baur, *Revolution and Tradition in Modern American Art* (Cambridge, Mass.: Harvard University Press, 1951), 48.

4 4   RUFINO TAMAYO   *The White Fruit Bowl*, 1938

The White Fruit Bowl was painted the year Rufino Tamayo was appointed art instructor at the Dalton School in New York City. For the next fifteen years he spent his winters in New York, establishing a prominent position for his art in the United States.

Still-life paintings of fruits are especially prominent in Tamayo's oeuvre. It has been suggested that this predilection may be attributed to Tamayo's experiences as a youth, working on his uncle's fruit farm and selling the produce in the market. Art historian James B. Lynch has written:

The sensuous properties of fruits constantly handled and savored undoubtedly appealed to . . . [Tamayo's] sensitive and passionate nature. Moreover the formal symmetry and . . . neatness of displays of produce must have gratified his strong . . . sense of order . . . [I]n this remembrance of things past, Tamayo discovered more than a favorite motif. He found a world of forms in harmony with Cézanne's prophetic vision: "You must see in nature, the cylinder, the sphere, and the cone."[1]

Tamayo's horizontal composition features a bunch of bananas, grapes, apples, and gourds arranged in a distinctive three-tiered bowl on the left, and, on the right, an empty bottle (which once contained a citrus drink) and several glasses with straws. Tamayo has unexpectedly inserted himself into the center of the composition by substituting his own name for the brand name on the label of the bottle (and also discretely indicating the date of the painting in the lower right corner of the label). But the most distinctive aspect of this painting is its subdued palette of white, blue, ocher yellow, pink, and terra-cotta. Through color, Tamayo sought to challenge stereotypical ideas about Mexican art and life:

Mexicans are not gay, as people think. In essence we are a very tragic people, who have been subdued again and again by outside forces. Our sadness . . . is expressed in our colors.[2]

He observes also that economic considerations sometimes predicate the choice of colors: in Mexico, earth colors are "the only ones the people can afford."[3]

Tamayo's celebration of aspects of Mexican culture associated with indigenous populations parallels similar interests on the part of his contemporaries, especially Diego Rivera and Frida Kahlo. Tamayo himself was a Zapotec and, as such, sought to declare his specifically "American" identity. Otherwise, however, he distanced himself from the more radical political tendencies of Rivera and the other major Mexican muralists, David Alfaro Siqueiros and José Clemente Orozco. Tamayo's ability to synthesize the cultural specificity of the Mexican art scene and the tenets of European modernism placed him in the forefront of the dialogue about mythic and totemic imagery in New York during the 1940s.[4]   LSS

1 James B. Lynch, *Tamayo*, exhib. cat. (Phoenix: Phoenix Art Museum, 1968), 14.
2 Emily Genauer, *Rufino Tamayo* (New York: Abrams, 1975), 31–32.
3 Ibid.
4 See Barnett Newman, "The Painting of Tamayo and Gottlieb" (1945), reprinted in John O'Neill, ed., *Barnett Newman: Selected Writings and Interviews* (New York: Alfred A. Knopf, 1990), 70–77.

45   A. E. GALLATIN   *Number 28 (Still Life)*, 1940

This painting is distinguished by the almost total abstraction of the still-life forms. Even the contours give almost no indication of the identity of the objects being depicted. Some readings of this composition see it as an easel setup, but a table arrangement is suggested by the setback of the dark brown area at the bottom left which forms a table edge and apron with the lighter brown band. The taupe areas at either side of the canvas suggest walls, and the pale yellow at the top may represent a window framed by dark brown bands. The forms on the table may be described as biomorphic. The curving tan shape at the bottom suggests a sheet of paper or a cloth, while the vertical gray and black forms that bisect the image are the most recognizable objects—a ruler and a T-square.

Gallatin is best known for his role as an adventurous supporter of the arts and an avant-garde aficionado in the period between the wars. Although he was trained as a lawyer, Gallatin's inheritance allowed him to cultivate an urbane lifestyle here and in Europe. He began collecting art in the early 1920s, and within a few years he had amassed an impressive collection of works by the School of Paris, French cubists, and young American modernists. In 1927 he installed his collection on the ground floor of New York University's main building on Washington Square (now the site of the Grey Art Gallery). The Gallery of Living Art (later called the Museum of Living Art) was on view until 1943. During its existence the gallery was one of the few places where young artists could see vanguard art from Europe and the United States.

As art historian Susan Larsen has written, "No artist was more indebted to the Cubist collection of the Gallery of Living Art than Gallatin himself."[1] His earliest work was done in Paris in the mid-1920s, and when he resumed painting in the 1930s after a ten-year hiatus, he turned to abstraction. As seen in this composition, Gallatin developed a rather competent interpretation of a synthetic cubist style, which he worked at from 1936 until his death in 1952. The influence of Léger on Gallatin's work has been noted by critics, but that of Juan Gris and Picasso is also evident. Gallatin was closely allied—both artistically and socially—with the abstract painters George K. L. Morris, Suzie Freylinghuysen, and Charles Shaw. He was also one of the first members of the American Abstract Artists Association, a group that promoted geometric abstraction in the United States before World War II.   LSS

1 Susan C. Larsen, "Albert Gallatin: The 'Park Avenue Cubist' Who Went Downtown," *Art News* 77 (December 1978): 982.

Franz Kline once explained his affinity with clowns by describing his own life as "a clown's tragedy."[1] He first demonstrated an interest in art in high school in Pennsylvania. While attending Boston University in the early 1930s, he also studied at the Boston Art Students League. In 1935 Kline traveled to England where he enrolled in Heatherley's School of Fine Art in London. He frequented the city's museums and galleries in search of subject matter. In 1938 he returned to the United States, eventually settling in New York City.

This still life was executed during Kline's early New York period, when he supported himself painting backdrops and murals for local nightclubs and taverns. The work was donated to the Metropolitan Museum by Kline's early patron, Dr. Theodore J. Edlich, Jr., who first met the artist in 1939. The combination of elements in this composition seems incongruous: a puppet dressed in formal attire and a top hat is slumped against several cans containing paint and brushes. These props rest atop an abruptly discarded canvas, surrounded by paint-stained rags and compressed tubes of paint. The objects in the background are even more nebulous: another canvas loosely suspended over an easel, the vinyl back of a chrome chair, and a diagonal buttress that extends from the wooden table on which the still life is set up.

During the 1930s and '40s Kline was especially influenced by the realist style of Reginald Marsh. Like Marsh, he sought his subjects in the streets of New York. But while Marsh tended to focus on the human figure, Kline was interested in individual objects. The strong gestural quality of Kline's early painting technique is noteworthy. Although he did not arrive at his fully abstract style until the 1950s, Kline seems to prefigure that later work in the bold black planes that sweep across this composition.

Whether or not Kline's admitted identification with the bittersweet existence of the clown was mere affectation, between 1936 and 1949 he painted a series of portraits of the famed Russian ballet dancer Nijinksy as the sad clown Petrushka, the victim of lost love. Art historian Harry F. Gaugh has noted that the puppet in this composition—one of several studies made by Kline in 1940s—has the same cocked-head pose as the Nijinsky portraits and may, therefore, relate to that series of paintings.[2] In an observation that might apply to this still life, painter and critic Elaine de Kooning said of Kline's Nijinsky portraits, "With the abject, blood-red eyes burning sadly in the pasty-white powered face, this painting fixes the star's private tragedy in his public image."[3] LSS

1 Harry F. Gaugh, "The Art of Franz Kline, 1930–1950: Figurative to Mature Abstraction" (Ph.D. diss., Indiana University, 1972), 2.
2 Ibid., 3
3 Elaine de Kooning, in *Franz Kline: Memorial Exhibition*, exhib. cat. (Washington, D.C.: Washington Gallery of Modern Art, 1962), 13.

4 7   Y A S U O   K U N I Y O S H I   *Broken Objects,* 1944

During a conversation with Whitney Museum curator Lloyd Goodrich in 1948, Japanese artist Yasuo Kuniyoshi talked about his still lifes. He explained that they were more than just painted objects and that they contained all kinds of veiled references.[1] *Broken Objects,* for example, is part of an unusual series of still lifes that refers to the artist's feelings during the last years of World War II.[2] For Kuniyoshi, the period after the Japanese bombing of Pearl Harbor in December 1941 was a difficult time. He was classified as an "enemy alien" by the U.S. government. His bank account was impounded, he had to report any trips he took, and his 35mm camera was confiscated.

On the tilted tabletop in *Broken Objects,* Kuniyoshi has laid out on a white cloth various objects that have been ripped or smashed. There is a glass ornament stuck into another glass, the broken lid of a cigar box, bits of brown cigar leaves, a torn-up black-and-white photograph of a nude woman, a green ribbon, and a pitcher draped with a red cloth and topped by a smashed vase. While the fragments in this still life place it in the tradition of memento mori paintings, the overall theme of the work is the destruction of objects that were once whole. Significantly, Kuniyoshi has substituted everyday things from his personal life for the more generic symbols normally featured in memento mori still lifes. The torn photograph of the nude woman, for instance, echoes a series of nude photographs Kuniyoshi took in 1939. That was also the year he separated from his second wife, Sara. The pitcher, familiar from other still lifes by Kuniyoshi, was one that he and Sara had purchased on their honeymoon in Mexico in 1935. SR

1 Lloyd Goodrich, "Notes on Conversation with YK," February 5, 1948, 3, Artist File, Whitney Museum of American Art Library.
2 Most of the information in this entry is from Tom Wolff, "Broken Objects," Artist File, Metropolitan Museum of Art.

Walter Murch was a gentle, retiring man who kept away from the hubbub of the New York art world. He lived on upper Riverside Drive in a studio cluttered with the objects he painted: bird carcasses, machine parts, gray rocks, dried onions, teapots, clockworks, broken dolls, architectural fragments, draperies, cut stone cubes, and spheres.[1] He is best known for his still lifes of machines, objects that he rendered poetic rather than merely mechanical. *Isotope* is an excellent example of Murch's mature style. It was painted as part of a series of cover illustrations commissioned by the magazine *Scientific American. Isotope* appeared on the cover of the March 1950 issue under the title *Hot Atom Chemistry.*

Seen at eye level and set against a bluish ground, this odd mechanical contraption seems like a slightly surreal monument against a blue sky. The grayish blue and soft tint of all the forms—as if they were seen through frosted glass—adds an incorporeal quality to this machine. The apparatus depicted here was actually used in the 1950s to handle radioactive materials. An isotope is one of two or more atoms that have the same number of protons but different numbers of neutrons.[2] Radioactive isotopes were often used as tracers in medical, biological, and industrial research since they could be followed, or traced, inside a plant or animal as it underwent various experiments. This process—the subject of Murch's painting—would be nearly invisible to a viewer. It is conducted in a bottle such as the one visible behind the little fortification of lead bricks used to protect the experimenter from the radioactive compound.

How was Murch able to depict this mechanical device in the first place? Apparently, after receiving the assignment, Murch was sent to Tracerlab, a Boston firm that made the instruments for isotope production. There, he selected from the many instruments those that he found visually stimulating, and they were sent to his New York studio so he could paint them.[3] Once they joined the poetic disorder of his Upper West Side studio, these scientific instruments probably just turned into evocative props.   S R

1 Cleve Grey, "Walter Murch: Modern Alchemist," *Art in America,* 51, no. 3 (March 1963): 81.
2 William Bridgewater and Elizabeth J. Sherwood eds., *Columbia Encyclopedia,* 2nd ed. (New York: Columbia University Press, 1950), 981.
3 Ernst W. Watson, "Walter Murch: Painter of the Impossible," *American Artist* 19, no. 8 (October 1955): 63.

California-born Carlyle Brown lived and worked for almost twenty years in Italy, settling in the town of Forio on the island of Ischia, just off the coast of Naples, in 1949. There, until his untimely death in 1964 at the age of forty-four, he concentrated on painting still-life arrangements of glasses, bottles, knives, scissors, eggs, and plates of fruit, as seen in this painting of 1952.

The dreamy, otherworldly ambiance of *Table with Figs and Lemons* indicates the lingering influence of Pavel Tchelitchew, who encouraged and supported Brown at the beginning of his career. Throughout this painting Brown has used subtle grayed yellow and green tonalities. The fact that the various objects seem to fade in and out of focus and occasionally leave a ghost image reveals Brown's thorough assimilation of cubist and futurist vocabularies. The sense of a fragile equilibrium is also emphasized by the fact that the artist has tilted the tabletop so that several of the objects seem on the verge of sliding off. A precariously perched spoon, a bit of twig, a knife, the mysteriously "hooded" bottle at the upper left, and the open scissors complete this surreal scenario.

The crisp rectangular folds of the linen napkin draped over the fruit bowl at the upper right are the only break in the symphony of ovals and circles. Another cloth has been carefully rolled around the prone wine bottle in the center, and at the lower right a paper has been unfolded to reveal the bunch of lemons. One lemon in particular breaks the revery of undisturbed perfection in the composition. Its pitted, greening surface is a reminder of the inevitable passage of time and the fragility of existence.

In addition to Tchelitchew, Brown counted Morris Graves among his mentors. (Graves spent the winter of 1948 with Brown and his wife in Siena.) It would also seem that Brown owed much to the example of the Italian metaphysical painter Giorgio Morandi. Despite the fact that his compositions are comparatively more cluttered than Morandi's, Brown's synthesis of cubist and classical values are comparable to that of the Italian master. Like Morandi, Brown proved his long-term fidelity to a limited repertoire of subjects, and succeeded in eliciting a sense of eternal values from the most humble objects.   LSS

At the age of twenty-three, Joseph Hirsch was awarded the Walter Lippincott Award for "the best figure painting in oil by an American citizen" at the Annual Exhibition of the Pennsylvania Academy of the Fine Arts. He earned a reputation for "socially oriented urban genre scenes," exemplified by his painting *The Room* (1958, Metropolitan Museum of Art). Such works indicate his artistic pedigree: study at the Pennsylvania Museum School of Industrial Art in Philadelphia (1928–31), with Henry Hensche in Provincetown, Massachusetts (summer 1935), and in 1932 with George Luks, a pioneer of socially relevant urban art at the beginning of the twentieth century.

At the same time Hirsch was involved in various political causes in the art world, and was a founding member and first treasurer of Artists Equity. Hired by the WPA Federal Art Project of Pennsylvania between 1939 and 1941, he painted murals for several public buildings in Philadelphia. From 1943 to 1944, he served as a war correspondent, documenting the activities of field personnel in the United States and North Africa. After World War II, Hirsch continued to be involved in painting and printmaking. He was a fourth-prize winner in the national competition *American Painting Today: 1950,* organized by the Metropolitan Museum of Art. An instructor at the Art Students League, New York, from 1959 to 1967, Hirsch was elected a member of the National Institute of Arts and Letters in 1967.[1] That Hirsch saw his own artistic mission as deviating from the main current of postwar abstract art is clear from a statement that he made in 1980:

When the critic wrote that one abstract painter closed the door, another pulled down the shade and the third turned out the light it was meant to be funny. It suggests that art must stay clear of all that is outside. Art is for the silence of the chapel, art is surcease from confrontation, from thought, from anguish, from blinding light. Art is "no comment." This is a grotesque notion.[2]

The presentation of fruits and various kitchen implements has been a familiar iconographic theme in still-life painting since the sixteenth century. Although this still life is titled *Melons,* it is really only one melon, a cantaloupe, from which a quarter has been sliced. The orange and taupe colors of the melon contrast with the blue plate on which the slice sits and the brown surface that serves as the tabletop. Despite Hirsch's impatience with abstract art, the depiction of these elements has been comfortably married with the more abstract delineation of the ground into successive bands of black, brown, white, and black. This structure tends to flatten the space in the painting, a sensation that is reinforced by the slightly awkward perspective of the knife, still lodged in the melon. However, one leg of the table emerges from the black shadows below to remind us of Hirsch's inherently realist predilection.   LSS

1 See *Joseph Hirsch,* exhib. cat. (Athens: Georgia Museum of Art, University of Georgia, 1970), n.p.; and Dorothy C. Miller, *Americans 1942: 18 Artists from 9 States,* exhib. cat. (New York: Museum of Modern Art, 1942), 60–66.
2 *Joseph Hirsch: Recent Paintings and Drawings,* exhib. cat. (New York: Kennedy Galleries, 1980), n.p.

Raymond Saunders has been described as "an American product: an intellectual with very rational reasons for trusting nothing but emotional coherence, a supremely skilled draftsman who loves to scribble, an intensely committed political artist whose work and life are full of optimism."[1] He has also been called "an abstract expressionist, a surrealist, a primitive, and an extremely influential father of graffiti art."[2] This painting amply demonstrates Saunders's adroit synthesis of a myriad of stylistic predilections into a highly personal idiom. *Something About Something* was executed in 1963, just two years after Saunders completed his M.F.A. at the California College of Arts and Crafts. Yet, already

in evidence are many of the elements that would later distinguish the artist's work—the Arshile Gorky-like drawing that inscribes abstract forms (seen in the "window" area at the upper right), the Willem de Kooning-like episodes of brushed color, and the Larry Rivers-like utilization of stenciled letters and numbers. Though influenced by other artists, Saunders ultimately had the skill to juxtapose abstraction with more empirical depiction and to make these disparate elements come together in visual concert.

Saunders's exquisite sense of texture is evident in the evocation of metal and glass (clear or multicolored and opaque) in still-life elements on the table. The use of black is also a distinctive feature of Saunders's work, and in *Something About Something* it is an essential component in constructing the "architecture" of the composition that surrounds the still life. Bulbous and round vases, a sweets tray, various glass containers, and yellow balls are set atop the horizontal expanse of black table and backdrop. Close examination reveals, however, that Saunders has actually used the black to obliterate, or mask, elements of the composition. The fields of black are also not monolithic. The black areas in the top half of the composition are veil-like, while the black wall beneath the still-life arrangement serves as a blackboard for miscellaneous doodlings. The lyricism of such passages in Saunders's work approaches that of Cy Twombly. Saunders has noticed the preoccupation of critics with his use of black in his compositions:

They say it's not a color. I say, look at [the work of] Monet. He painted his experience. That's not something you see, it's something you realize. It's feeling the color, being the color. They say black's not a color? I say, Hey! What about me?[3] LSS

1 Jim Quinn, "Art Lessons," *Philadelphia Inquirer Magazine* (February 25, 1990): 32.
2 Ibid.
3 Ibid., 29.

Kitchens are rare settings for still-life paintings, except, of course, their original popularity in seventeenth-century Dutch genre scenes. Not surprisingly, even today, such purely functional environments complete with sinks, stoves, and refrigerators awake little inspiration in artists. By contrast, such masters as Edgar Degas and Pierre Bonnard have transformed other, equally improbable places, such as bathrooms outfitted with tubs and mirrors, into magical settings for their depictions of erotic nudes and bathers. *Fay's Kitchen* refers to a kitchen less by its specific attributes than by allusion. On a counter, just below eye level, the artist has placed a salt shaker and a shiny paint can. Apparently, he painted the two objects from life but he "invented the counter, wall and shadows." He then arranged the objects to create "a syncopated rhythm of shadow, object, shadow, object, shadow."[1]

Actually, with the light coming from the right foreground, only the large shadow cast on the wall by the can of paint can be explained. The other shadows, on both the right and the left, are formal inventions. In this austere setting, an otherwise ubiquitous paint can becomes the main focus. The shiny metal surface of the can forms an iridescent abstract design that dominates the entire composition. Its bent shape also acts as a distorting mirror. Within its marbleized pattern can be glimpsed a reduced reflection of the salt shaker. Drips of white opaque paint on top of the can add to the design. Although a can of paint and a salt shaker might appear to be incongruous staples in a kitchen, both objects seem to have been chosen more for their surface qualities of translucency and reflection.

As to the person called Fay referred to in the homespun title, she does not exist. As the artist later explained, by 1971, the date of this painting, he was completing his M.F.A. degree at the University of California at Davis. When he prepared his final exhibition at the University he decided—in the punning spirit of the time—to title all of his works either "Emma" or "Fay," which rhymes phonetically with M.F.A.   SR

1 Chuck Forsman, Artist's Statement, (February 6, 1988), Object Record Sheet, Departmental Archive, 20th Century Art Department, Metropolitan Museum of Art.

Curator Linda Cathcart has described Paul Wonner's approach to still-life painting as similar to landscape painting because of his tendency to divide his compositions horizontally.[1] In *"Dutch" Still Life with Orchids, Postcard View of Paris, and "Death of Marat"* he has set down side-by-side six floral arrangements in a variety of containers. From left to right we see an orchid plant in a used can of Campbell's tomato juice; another tall orchid in a San Miguel beer bottle; and a tulip, pink camellia, sprig of yellow freesia, and a clump of flowering rosemary in a double-handled blue vase. At the center of the composition an arced stalk of purple cybidium orchids rises out of a wine carafe set on a long-legged table. Next to that is a bunch of daffodils set in a blue-and-white Delft vase, signifying Wonner's homage to seventeenth-century Dutch still-life painting. The vase balances precariously atop a used paint can, a cardboard box, and a wooden crate. To the extreme right, just making it into the composition, is a branch of phaelonopsis orchids in a wine bottle.[2]

In this painting, Wonner engages a number of artistic strategies: updating the "botanical realist" still life, trompe l'oeil illusionism, and a pop-art interest in commercial logos and labeling. While the formal organization and attention to botanical details seem to indicate careful calculation in composing this work, Wonner actually develops his compositions quite spontaneously. As he explains:

I first set a background and a "floor plan," then paint the objects separately . . . not arranged ahead of time. I seldom know what will come next, and the final result is always somewhat of a surprise to me.[3]

He delights in the "subjective linear designs" that develop as "each object or shadow [leads] to another throughout the painting."[4] The structure of the composition is determined by the interplay between horizontal and vertical elements, against which are set the diagonals of the shadow lines, the alignment of the cardboard box, the sheet of paper (on which the artist has signed and dated the painting), and the green pencil. Within the pervasive stillness, Wonner has introduced small indications of the passage of time: two blooms have fallen from the purple cybidium orchid, several daffodils show wear, and the tulip is well past its prime.

Wonner often inserts books, greeting cards, and postcard images into his paintings. They seem to function both as spatial devices within the overall composition, as well as art historical reference points for Wonner's artistic ambitions. The artist would probably account for the presence of the view of the Seine River in Paris, and of the well-known composition *Death of Marat*, by the eighteenth-century French painter Jacques-Louis David, as one of the consequences of his unpremeditated pictorial composing.

A native of Arizona, Wonner studied art at the California College of Arts and Crafts in Oakland from 1937 to 1941. After spending several years in New York City during the late 1940s, he returned to California to complete his graduate work at the University of California in Berkeley in 1953. Although he then became associated with the Bay Area figurative painters—David Park, Elmer Bischoff, and Richard Diebenkorn—by the mid-1960s, Wonner was working almost exclusively on still-life compositions.   L S S

1 Linda Cathcart, *American Still Life, 1945–83,* exhib. cat. (Houston: Contemporary Art Museum, 1983), 138.
2 I am grateful to Ben Feiman, Assistant Manager, Buildings Department, The Metropolitan Museum of Art, for help in identifying flowers in this composition.
3 *Paul Wonner,* exhib. cat. (New York: Hirschl and Adler Modern, 1983), 5.
4 Ibid.

"That birthday party ended in a fight," might be one's initial reaction to the broken crockery on the table. Yet a closer look reveals that the smashed cups, saucers, and plates have been strategically placed, some of them in an upright position. In fact, the debris-strewn table never served as a festive banquet. Instead, Valerio set up the monumental still life as a fictitious challenge to some artist—himself, as it turned out—about "to come in and take it on."[1] The chosen medium could be canvas or paper—both are set up, one on the easel in the background, the other on the small drawing horse in the foreground.

Valerio says he conceived this complex picture after painting a small still life of a box containing broken bits of china. Inspired by the elaborate effects that painting produced, he began setting up this unusual still life on a large table in his dark, wood-paneled studio downstairs. In a playful mood he chose objects that would simulate water themes: the folds of the luxurious red, flower-patterned textile on the left imitate waves; the upright dishes mime the fins of fish; the tawdry turquoise comb alludes to a fish's skeleton; and the crystal bowl is like a jellyfish. For good measure, he added the duck decoy. The strong overhead light creates brilliant reflections on the glass and crystal, further highlighting the painter's mastery of his medium. And finally, two mirrors multiply the visual space, duplicating many of the objects. Valerio works from both the actual setup and Ektachromes of it. Here, although he worked mostly from color transparencies, he kept the elaborate table set up in his studio for reference.

When asked about the meaning of this painting, Valerio referred to the white-frosted chocolate cake in the center of the image and said he wanted to "have his cake and eat it, too."[2] In other words, this still life gave him the license to explore actual and dream space, reality and metaphor, all in one composition. The artist's own summary of the daunting task is captured in the brand name of a cigar inscribed on the open lid of a box in the foreground—*El Producto*, "It's quite a production."[3]   S R

1 John Valerio, conversation with author, August 24, 1995.
2 Ibid.
3 Ibid.

5 5   AMY WEISKOPF   *Still Life with Clock,* 1986

"I spent a long time working out this composition, arranging and rearranging the objects," says Amy Weiskopf.[1] She was in Rome when she composed this still life in 1986, and had just finished graduate school. Inspired by the work of the Renaissance masters that she was seeing in Italy, she chose the vanitas theme for this painting. It contains only objects that relate to the passage of time. In vanitas still lifes, skulls, burning candles, and hourglasses serve as allegorical reminders of the transience of time and the vanity of human endeavors. In this work, Weiskopf assembled everyday objects with a similar symbolic value: a deck of tarot cards and a mathematician's ruler, an old wind-up clock from a local shop, three large dried maple leaves and three gourds. Strangely enough, the white gourd visible through the swung-open glass of the off-kilter clock is not magnified by the thick glass. But what is the meaning of these gourds that hang from strings like plumb bobs? They are also symbols of transience, the artist says: "After a while they are going to rot and fall off."[2] After Weiskopf had arranged these objects to her satisfaction, for the next two months, day after day, she painstakingly painted this reminder of time.   SR

1 Amy Weiskopf, conversation with author, June 21, 1995.
2 Ibid.

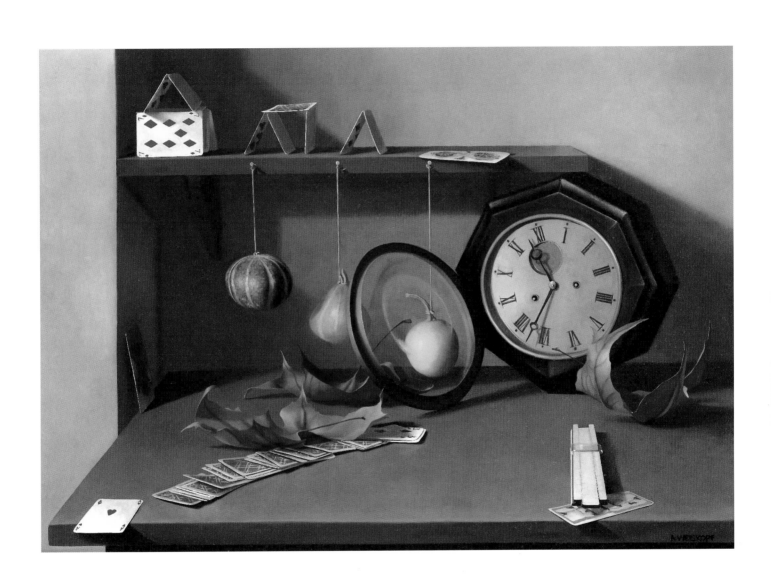

THE ICONIC OBJECT

From the end of the Greco-Roman era through the Renaissance, still-life elements appeared in European painting as accompaniments to the main image. Fruit, foodstuffs, musical instruments, and utensils served as iconographic markers, enhancing the reading of the composition with symbolic meaning. In the sixteenth and seventeenth centuries, however, still life flowered as an independent, secular category of painting. Individual elements were combined in compositions to convey readings that not only reflected man's celebration of the material world and worldly possessions but also the futility of their pursuit in the long run.

It is interesting to note, therefore, how in the twentieth century the presentation of an individual object came to be an end in itself of still-life painting. As art historian Ellen Johnson has observed:

The entire gamut of modern art can be viewed from the vantage point of the artist's attitude towards the object, an examination which should throw some light on the larger problem of how the modern artist chooses to interweave art and reality and ultimately what constitutes reality for him.[1]

The paintings in this section present single objects as diverse as a clamshell, a wreath, a horn, a box, a doll's head, a heart, a hammer and sickle, a hot cup of liquid, and a close-up of the head of a cadaver. They show a variety of painterly techniques—from Georgia O'Keeffe's pristine rendering of the clamshell (cat. no. 57), to the expressionistic texturing of Aaron Fink's presentation of a steaming cup of coffee (cat. no. 62). This variety of interpretations makes clear that the individual artist's approach to the act of painting is as important as what he or she paints. Johnson describes this tension as "the painted object . . . and the object painted [vying] with each other for dominance."[2]

Consequently, the objects in these paintings are not merely vehicles for displaying stylistic virtuosity; they are also purveyors of meaning. Political metaphor, for example, is found in Warhol's *Still Life* (cat. no. 59), which puns on the symbol of Russian communism with trademarked products of the capitalist system. Jim Dine's painting *The Heart, South of Naples* (cat. no. 61) shows how this central form serves as a surrogate for an individual or a relationship. Joe Andoe's *Untitled (Wreath)* (cat. no. 63) and *Untitled (Horn)* (cat. no. 64) present single, iconic symbols and images similar to those found on eighteenth- and nineteenth-century American furniture, samplers, and architectural embellishments. Marsden Hartley's *The Virgin of Guadalupe* (cat. no. 56) and Audrey Flack's *Macarena of Miracles* (cat. no. 58) are depictions of other representations (in both cases statues of the Virgin Mary) and therefore call into question the relationship between reality and artifice.

Robert Cumming's *Burning Box* (cat. no. 65) was inspired by a medieval wooden container that the artist saw in a museum in Amsterdam. His painting of the box, meaningful in itself, has been decorated with words and motifs that also demand decoding. And finally, two very different paintings deal with the subject of death: Jerome Witkin's *Number 4818* (cat. no. 60) is a close-up of the head of a cadaver, rendered an object by the flight of the life force; and James Rosenquist's extreme close-up of the plastic head of a *Gift Wrapped Doll #16* (cat. no. 66), which constitutes the artist's statement about the AIDS epidemic.   LSS

1 Ellen H. Johnson, *Modern Art and the Object* (New York: Harper & Row Publishers, 1996), 11.
2 Ibid., 12.

A key figure in the artistic circle around the photographer and gallery owner Alfred Stieglitz, Marsden Hartley adapted cubism to his own personal use before turning to a more expressive figural style after World War I. In his search to find a uniquely American art that would combine a modernist vocabulary with a regionalist flavor, Hartley looked to the southwestern United States for inspiration. Like artists John Marin and Georgia O'Keeffe, he settled in Taos, New Mexico, which, along with Santa Fe, had become the center for a vibrant colony of artists and writers between the two world wars. Although he stayed in New Mexico for only a year (1918–19), the visual memory of the landscape and culture would continue to inspire Hartley's work through the mid-1920s.

This painting of a statue of the Virgin of Guadalupe, a popular religious icon in the Southwest and in Mexico, was one of the works Hartley finished while he was actually in New Mexico.[1] The story of the Virgin of Guadalupe dates back to the sixteenth century, when an Indian named Juan Diego saw a vision of the Virgin on a hill northwest of Mexico City. According to the story, the Virgin told Juan Diego to have the local bishop build a church on the site of the vision. The bishop refused to believe his story. Three days later the Virgin appeared again and instructed Juan Diego to pick some flowers and take them to the bishop. When Juan Diego opened his mantle to present the roses to the bishop, an image of the Virgin could be seen beneath: the Virgin's communication with Juan Diego was verified. The devotion to the Virgin of Guadalupe then became a uniquely New World manifestation, providing a more indigenous access to Catholicism.[2]

In this image of the Virgin of Guadalupe, Hartley adheres rather closely to traditional representations. She stands on a crescent moon, supported on the head of an angel, her hands folded in prayer. The rays emanating from her body and the scalloped border are also part of the image preserved in the sanctuary at Guadalupe. The rough-hewn generalization of form, the flat design, and the bold primary colors are consistent with the stylistic character of Hartley's work at the time. The details of his depiction of the Virgin of Guadalupe represent an adaption of Spanish high baroque religious sculpture, which often featured polychromed surfaces and actual costuming of the statuary (as seen in Audrey Flack's *Macarena of Miracles* [cat. no. 58]). As an added still-life element, Hartley has inexplicably included a banana—which mimics the shape of the crescent moon— two pears and an apple.   L S S

1 See Patricia Janis Broder, *The American West: The Modern Vision* (Boston: Little, Brown and Co., 1984), 134–44.
2 See *New Catholic Encyclopedia*, vol. 6 (New York: McGraw-Hill, 1967), 821.

Every summer during the 1920s, Georgia O'Keeffe visited York Beach, Maine. As was her habit, she focused on aspects of that environment as a source of subject matter for her art. Seashells left on the beach by the tides inspired several compositions, of which this was the last. In this painting of the interior of one half of a clamshell, O'Keeffe presents what art historian Lisa Messinger describes as a "magnified" image.[1] With no definition of the exterior contour, the extreme close-up of the inner structure of the shell eliminates a sense of scale or identity. Moreover, the interior is cast in a brilliant light so that the concavity of the shell actually seems flat. The nuances of the shell begin to look like a landscape: the inward-sloping crevices which extend to the joint suggest the opening of a cave and the gentle swells in the middle approximate rolling hills. Scholars have remarked on similar effects in the work of photographer Edward Weston, an associate of O'Keeffe's husband, Alfred Stieglitz. Weston's own closely observed views of mundane objects provoke an unexpected sense of monumental scale and abstract illusion.[2] O'Keeffe's earlier paintings of shells presented the two halves set on edge, making their allusions to human physiognomy quite explicit.

Painted in 1930 as a memento of O'Keeffe's time at York Beach, this image may also allude to the artist's recent discovery of New Mexico. Indeed, the extreme monochromatism and simplicity of forms in this painting are comparable to O'Keeffe's *Ranchos Church* (1930, Metropolitan Museum of Art), a study of the eighteenth-century church in Taos that she painted that same year. O'Keeffe's subsequent paintings, particularly her studies of the mountains and mesas of New Mexico, are less ambiguous than *Clam Shell.* This was undoubtedly to discourage the extravagantly Freudian readings of sexual content in her work by New York critics in the 1920s.[3]   L S S

1 Lisa Mintz Messinger, *Georgia O'Keeffe* (New York and London: Thames and Hudson and The Metropolitan Museum of Art, 1988), 38.
2 Ibid., 24–25, 30–31, 42.
3 See Charles Child Eldredge III, "Georgia O'Keeffe: The Development of an American Modern" (Ph.D. diss., University of Minnesota, 1971), 50–51.

5 8   AUDREY FLACK   *Macarena of Miracles,* 1971

Audrey Flack is one of the best-known photorealist painters. As seen in this depiction of a seventeenth-century Spanish Baroque sculpture, her work focuses on the relationship between photographic recording and painterly depiction. It is also a collaboration of a sort between two women artists, who have each used their art to address their spiritual well-being.

This particular apparition of the Virgin Mary is known as the Macarena Esperanza and is the patron saint of the city of Seville. It was carved by Luisa Roldan, one of the earliest known women artists in Spain. In the seventeenth century, such statues were the object of intense devotion and ritual. Customarily, the wooden sculpture was polychromed, then dressed in an actual costume of sumptuous fabrics and lace, elaborately festooned with gold, pearls, and precious gems. This high baroque style was later transported to the Americas and, as seen in Marsden Hartley's 1919 painting *The Virgin of Guadalupe* (cat. no. 56), continued to have currency well into the twentieth century.

The intense physicality of Roldan's statue, captured well in Flack's painting, is characteristic of the art produced under the Catholic Church during the Counter-Reformation. The intention was to make the spiritual presence of the Virgin, the angels, and the saints as dramatic and real as possible in order to reinforce the connection between the faithful and the church. Flack has used an airbrush to reproduce the surface nuances of the polychromed figure. But for all her close scrutiny of surface and texture, there is nary a blemish to be seen here. Any incidental records of the passage of time—fraying of the costume, cracking of the surface veneer—has been banished from this image. Flack worked from photographs of the sculpture taken shortly after the 1970 trip to Spain when she first encountered the work of Luisa Roldan. LSS

During a visit to Italy in 1976, Warhol became intrigued by the hammer-and-sickle symbols that he saw everywhere. The communist emblem seemed to be a ready-made pop icon. At the time, the hammer and sickle was most familiar from the flag of the Soviet Union. The crossed tools were meant to symbolize the union of industrial and agricultural workers under communism. But for Warhol, the very ubiquity of the symbol made it lose its political meaning. As he explained at the time, "Gee, when you walk around in Italy, all over the walls no matter where you go, there's in chalk or print, there's all these images scribbled on everything with hammer and sickle."[1]

When he returned to New York, Warhol asked his assistant Ronnie Cutrone to find him an image of the hammer and sickle, but in three dimensions to add the play of shadows. Over the next three weeks Cutrone haunted the city's communist stores but was unable to find a three-dimensional image. So Warhol decided to use real objects. Cutrone went to the Astro Hardware Center near the artist's studio on Union Square and bought a double-headed hammer and a sickle, the latter prominently labeled "Champion No. 15/b True Temper." These objects were posed in different configurations and photographed under different lighting setups. From these photographs, Warhol produced a series of

paintings, drawings, watercolors, and prints in which these tools lie in various poses of disarray. In some works, the hammer stands upright on its head, while the sickle is propped against a vertical plane. This large version represents a gigantic close-up of the bright red hammer and sickle; the shadows rival the objects in prominence. Fittingly, in these "tool" paintings Warhol resurrected the brilliant red and white colors of his famous Campbell's soup can paintings.

When these still lifes were unveiled at the Leo Castelli Gallery in Soho in 1977—the artist had not shown his work in New York since 1966—the public reacted with both surprise and revulsion. Reviewers were confused about the artist's motives. Ever elusive, Warhol told one interviewer: "Everybody's always asked me if I am a communist because I've done Mao. So now I'm doing hammer and sickles for communism and skulls for fascism."[2]   S R

1 Patrick S. Smith, *Andy Warhol's Art and Films* (Ann Arbor: UMI Research Press, 1981), 278.
2 Ibid., 585, n. 31.

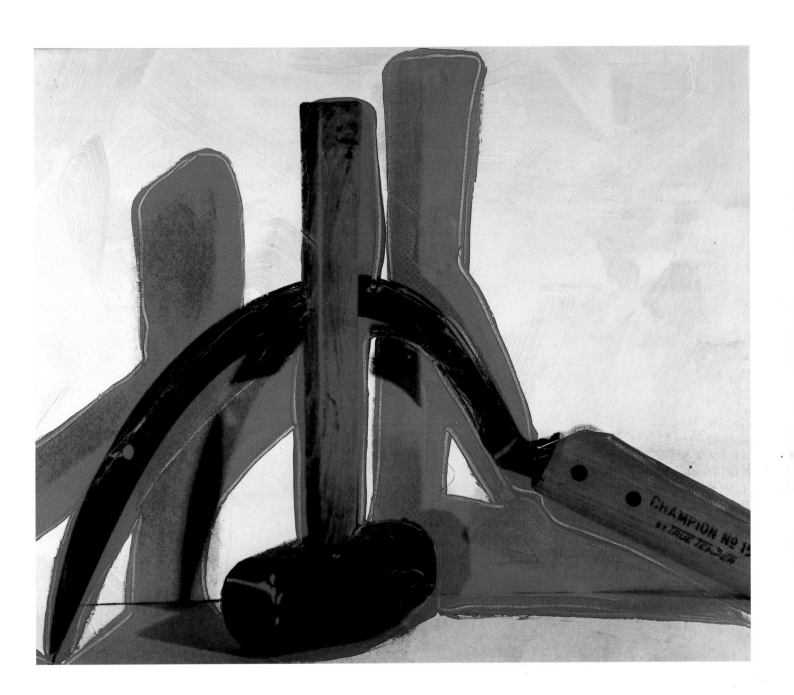

Over the last two decades, Jerome Witkin has captured aspects of modern life that are as stark and unromanticized as this depiction of a dead body in a morgue. The spare expressionism of this composition reveals the artist's special affinity to the work of artists such as Grunewald, Goya, and Caravaggio, who, in their own times, were known for their uncompromising visions. Witkin has written, "Like Goya, I believe that an artist must know and respond to the life around him, including the darkest places."[1]

Here, Witkin shows a detail of a dead body laid out on a steel table, its neck and shoulders propped up on a wooden block. The eyes are empty cavities, and the mouth opens wordless, breathless. Evidence of the evisceration of the autopsy is seen in the exposed chest cavity and musculature of the head and shoulders. Witkin's painting was executed several years earlier than Andres Serrano's morgue photographs, but in both cases the artists allude to changes that death brings each of us. In their objectifications of the human body they record the transition of the figure from a life that has been stilled to a still life.[2]

We do not know how this person died, but the designation by a number—4818—suggests an anonymous demise and the autopsy implies a suspicious one. Witkin accentuates the dramatic aspect of this scenario by making the space as dungeon-like as possible. We see the bare brick wall and the grated floor (to facilitate disposition of bodily fluids). These grim details contrast sharply with the visual impact of Serrano's lush color photographs. In the words of curator Richard Porter:

From abstract expressionism Witkin retains the vitality that gives such impact to his canvases, which are built up in a symphonic performance of heavily laden brushstrokes that seem to be both palpable and audible. Revealed by harsh electric lights, hot oranges clangor against garish greens, and push reds and purples to a crescendo of color. This concept of pictures as performance is essential to a painter who credits the gestural abstractionist Willem de Kooning with having as much to do with his technical development as such old masters as Hals, Velásquez, and Goya.[3]   LSS

1 Gerrit Henry, *Jerome Witkin: Moral Visions,* exhib. cat. (Richmond: Marsh Gallery, University of Richmond, 1986), 5.
2 A 1986 group exhibition at the Sherry French Gallery in New York which included this painting was entitled *Still Life: Life That Is Still.*
3 Richard Porter, *Jerome Witkin, A Decade of Work: Paintings and Drawings,* exhib. cat. (University Park: Museum of Art, The Pennsylvania State University, 1983), 7.

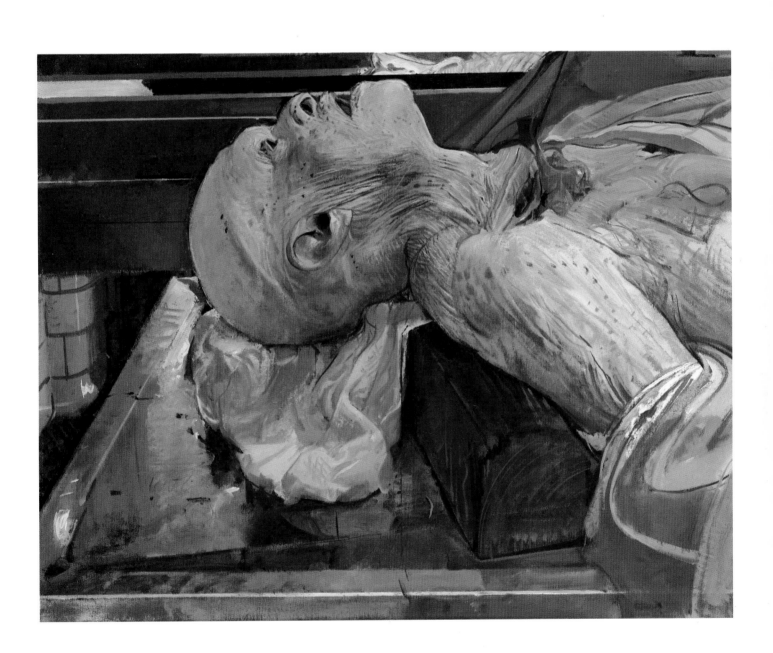

Although Jim Dine was one of the key figures in pop art in the 1960s, he always maintained a distinctive position within that artistic movement. While he engaged everyday objects and images like his contemporaries Warhol, Lichtenstein, and Oldenburg, Dine has consistently approached these forms symbolically. He himself has noted that he is "too subjective" to be really considered part of the pop art movement:

Pop is concerned with exteriors, I'm concerned with interiors. *When I use objects, I see them as a vocabulary of feelings. . . . I think it's important to be autobiographical.*[1]

The heart has been a signature motif for Jim Dine for three decades. This large image of a heart is based on standardized renderings from commercial imagery and features painterly episodes that display Dine's appreciation for gestural abstraction. The heart is suspended in a brilliant blue field. Inside the heart are bursts and rills of reds, yellows, and oranges, which are balanced by the gray colors at the edges. At the bottom of the composition is a panoply of sea life—snails, lobsters, two or three species of fish, perhaps a shark and a squid. While such iconic emblems are not normally associated with still-life painting, *The Heart, South of Naples* demonstrates how Dine has overturned the genre's "detached mood" and its "somber reckoning of palpable things."[2]

As is his custom, Dine recycles elements in his work, treating them as a basic vocabulary that can be reused and recombined in new contexts. Both the heart form and the sea life appear in another series of paintings by Dine titled "Atheism," also from 1986. A 1985 drawing entitled *Pompeiian Heart* also features the heart surrounded by sea life. And finally, a more autobiographical use of the heart shape—this time in relation to tools—is Dine's *Crommelynck Gate with Tools* (1983, Metropolitan Museum of Art), a dual homage to his father and his printer in Paris, Aldo Crommelynck.

Dine's use of the heart motif stems from a 1965 commission from the Actors' Workshop in San Francisco to paint the stage set for a production of Shakespeare's *A Midsummer Night's Dream*. Since then, Dine has explored this imagery in painting, prints, and sculpture. He has rendered the heart in straw, sheet metal, wire, and rope. At times the symbol refers to his state of mind, at other times it alludes to personal relationships, and at still others it serves as a homage to artists Dine admires. In his hands the heart has proven capable of surprising versatility and range.[3]   L S S

1 John Gruen, "Jim Dine and the Life of Objects," *Art News* 76, no. 7 (September 1977), 38.
2 Carter Ratcliff, *Jim Dine: New Paintings,* exhib. cat. (New York: Pace Gallery, 1988), n.p.
3 See Graham Beal, *Jim Dine: Five Themes,* exhib. cat. (New York: Abbeville Press in association with the Walker Art Center, 1984), 36–40.

For some, this steaming cup might evoke a faded advertisement high up on an outside wall. Such ghosts from the past can sometimes be glimpsed on deteriorating walls in large cities. Often they are brought to light—in relatively fresh colors, but with scumbled surfaces—on walls laid bare by demolition.

Aaron Fink is a Boston-based artist who has exhibited his work for the last fifteen years. From the beginning of his career, he kept his stock imagery to a bare minimum: a peanut, a plum, a grape, a cherry, a lemon, a red apple, a face or a flame. Magnified against a black ground, these simple elements defy their mundane, daily associations. They assume the gigantic and out-of-scale proportions that amazed Lemuel Gulliver during his visit to Brobdingnag, the land populated by giants in Swift's satirical masterpiece *Gulliver's Travels* (1726).

Fink severs all links to the iconography of pop art—magnified, pristine images of consumer items such as soup cans or Coca-Cola bottles—by giving a worn look to the surface of his paintings. He creates the puckered passages of his painting surfaces by a method called counterproofing. Fink presses a sheet of paper against the wet canvas and then pulls the image off it. He then scratches a grid over his painted images to serve as "a reminder that the surface of the painting is two-dimensional."[1]

The theme of the steaming cup—this is part of an entire series of oils and counterproofs on paper—came to Fink during a trip to Paris in the fall of 1982. As the artist describes it:

One evening I was sitting at a sidewalk café having a cup of coffee. At that time in Paris all the automobile headlights were foglight yellow. The effect of the white coffee cup, and everything else for that matter, being bathed in this strange yellow light really struck me. When I returned to my studio I began to work on the first of the cup paintings. These early ones were painted only in black and yellow in the attempt to permeate the canvas with that yellow light as I remembered it. As I continued to work with and develop the image of the cup it changed, more colors were added, the steam became a prominent feature, in certain paintings a spoon is resting in the saucer. Through all of this the light in the painting became less and less yellow, but the color of the cup has remained yellow.[2]

The idea of the picture may have been born in a café in Paris but the directness and energy of the image appear distinctly American, not least in the bold pattern of the red-and-white steam which evokes the fluttering stripes of the U.S. flag.   S R

1 Aaron Fink, letter to author, September 15, 1993.
2 Ibid.

"I tend to economize," the artist explains, "I want to reduce images to their blueprint."[1] Indeed, the beguiling simplicity of the objects in Joe Andoe's paintings evokes images found in school primers. Continuing this analogy, the words "Wreath" and "Horn" could be imagined in the spots where the artist has now placed his signature. Andoe strives for an utter distillation of image, ground, and color in his work. Not surprisingly, then, his inventory of subjects remains basic: horns, wreaths, candles, flowers, cornstalks, trees, cattle, buffaloes, lambs, sheep, and, lately, horses.

Mentally prepared, but without a preparatory design, he begins with a blank canvas. He applies a layer of gesso to the canvas, sometimes in a spiraling motion as in *Untitled (Horn)*, sometimes with vertical and horizontal strokes as in *Untitled (Wreath)*. Once the gesso has dried, he uses a palette knife to apply a thin layer of oil paint, building up the layers in certain places, and leaving other places with only a thin wash of color. In *Untitled (Wreath)*, he scratched the design of the flowers and grains of wheat directly into the wet surface with the end of his brush.

Andoe is bent on creating pared-down, timeless, and generic images, an attitude that extends to his use of a monochromatic, earth-colored ground. "By using earth colors, I further distill my images to next to nothing," he says.[2] Similarly, Andoe likes his objects to subtly fuse with the background. In *Untitled (Wreath)* the dark brown flowers and grains of wheat that alternate around the wreath are barely distinguished from their murky, black-brown background. Likewise, in *Untitled (Horn)*, painted in shades of umber and browns, the horn is a pale, hovering shape that has barely any substance at all, particularly compared to the solid brown band above it and the narrow strip of landscape below.

Andoe's upbringing in a fundamentalist Christian family in Tulsa, Oklahoma, has led some critics to infer that his images derive from the Bible, a suggestion the artist rejects. When he came to New York in 1982, during the fashion for neoexpressionism, nobody was interested in his hushed images. He made ends meet by supporting himself and his family with construction work. His luck turned in 1987, when the Swiss dealer Thomas Ammann discovered his paintings in the back room of a New York gallery, where they were being stored temporarily. Recognition, a permanent dealer, and exhibitions followed almost magically. S R

1 Joe Andoe, conversation with author, June 27, 1995.
2 Ibid.

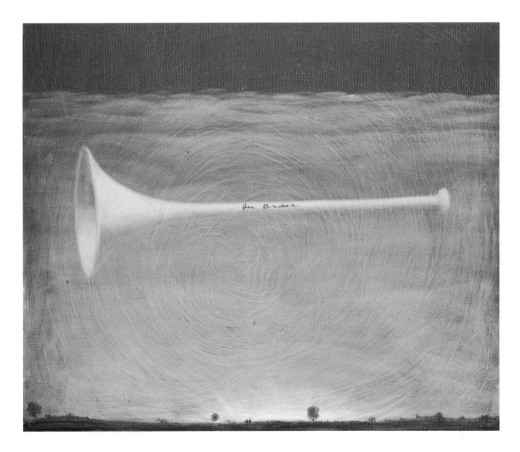

The inspiration for this work was a medieval wooden box the artist admired in a museum in Amsterdam. All the artist can now remember was that "it was smaller than a sewing machine, but larger than a shoebox."[1] Dating from about A.D. 1000, the box was painted in white, red, and black. What most intrigued Cumming about it, however, were the "strange, scroll-like things painted around it, they looked like flames . . . I found it ironic that this wooden object had been 'burning' for hundreds of years (yet not consumed) . . . since the artist had rendered it."[2] From sketches he jotted in his small black notebook on site, the artist later made half a dozen versions of "box pictures," of which this is one.

With the precise manner of a mechanical draftsman, Cumming has delineated the two objects—the rectangular box above and the gate below—both surrounded by flames. The words "box," "burning," and "gate" are printed on the canvas. The juxtaposition of these two recognizable but unrelated objects provokes questions about the artist's intention. Could the box be read as a small house? Or as a coffin? Does the gate lead to purgatory? Or to the furnace of a crematory? These morbid associations are counterbalanced by references to folk art in the draftsmanlike precision of the design, the decorative colorful patterning, and the artist's selfmade saw-toothed wooden frame.

The connections between abstract thought, the written word, and artistic representation have fueled Cumming's work since the late 1960s. His oeuvre is vast and includes paintings, drawings, prints, sculpture, photographs, and books. Several large-scale watercolors preceded this thinly washed oil painting. Like much of his recent work, *Burning Box* is a perplexing combination of technical precision and painterly expression. S R

1 Robert Cumming, conversation with author, June 28, 1995.
2 Robert Cumming, Artist's Statement, April 22, 1991, Object Record Sheet, Departmental Archive, 20th Century Art Department, Metropolitan Museum of Art.

Since the 1960s James Rosenquist has drawn on his experiences painting backdrops for department stores and commercial billboards to create powerful paintings that comment on the American scene. This composition is from a series of paintings—all close-ups of the heads of plastic-wrapped dolls, all measuring five feet square—executed in 1992–93. The artist titled the series "The Serenade for the Doll After Claude Debussy" or "Gift Wrapped Dolls." The depiction of the dolls in this series is as fascinating as it is morbid. The wide-eyed stare of the doll— conveying a hyperalertness and liveliness— seems at odds with our empathetic experience of suffocation provoked by the obsessively detailed rendering of its plastic covering. Despite his straightforward appropriation of a photographic image, Rosenquist cultivates a highly abstract style in delineating the elaborately wrought folds and sheen of the plastic wrapping. At times pulled taut, at times striated on the vertical, the wrapping responds to the serendipity of the weight, position, and form of each doll. The result is an all-over play of highlights that distort and at times obliterate our view of the doll heads beneath. The "natural" coloring of the dolls is also distorted by the colors that reflect off the glossy surface of the plastic. In this painting, for instance, a pervasive red floods the right-hand side, transforming

the doll into a garish harridan. This effect is further enhanced by the distortion of the view of her left eye, which seems to become an empty, pupilless void.

Rosenquist has commented that dolls have always appeared "stark or scary" to him, especially "the fifties doll with the anonymous face and a wide blank stare" depicted in this series.[1] Accordingly, his tight focus on the heads of these dolls has transformed an otherwise banal object, wrapped for display, into a portent of psychological horror. That horror, according to the artist, is the AIDS epidemic. In a statement for the catalogue of the exhibition of the "Gift Wrapped Dolls," Rosenquist noted his concern about the future of children and their ability to form relationships because of AIDS: "The coolness, the thoughtfulness that will be in a young romance make it seem the complete antithesis of passion."[2]   LSS

1 James Rosenquist, interview with David Whitney, in *James Rosenquist: The Serenade for the Doll After Debussy, or Gift Wrapped Dolls & Masquerade of the Military Industrial Complex Looking Down on the Insect World,* exhib. cat. (New York: Leo Castelli Gallery, 1993), 5.
2 Ibid.

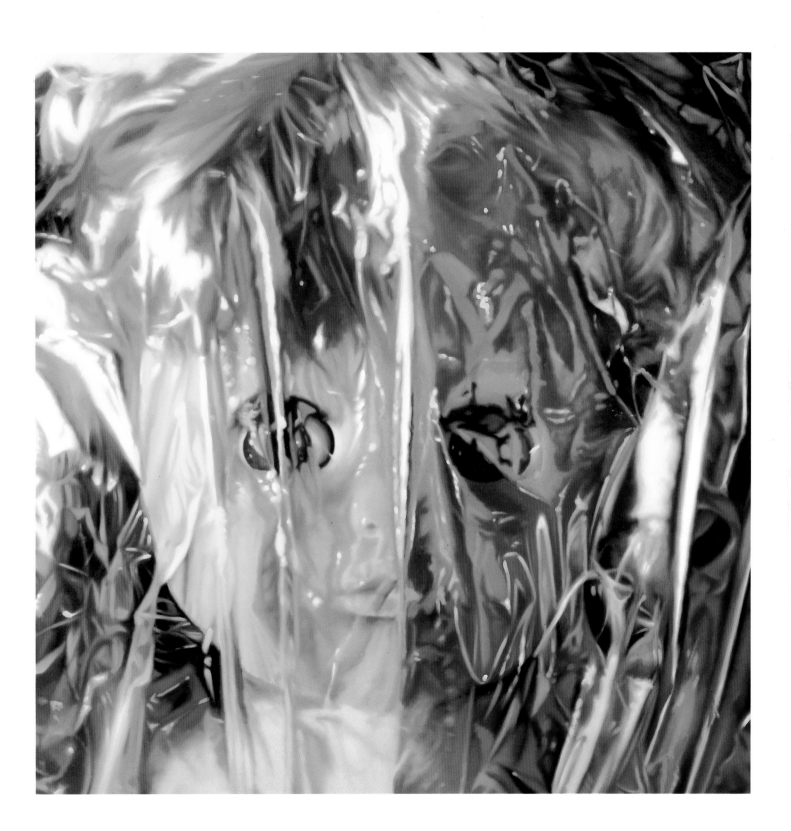

CHECKLIST OF THE EXHIBITION

TERRY ALLEN B. 1943

The Prisoner Song, 1984
Pencil and colored pencil on paper, oil, lead
strips, gum, Plexiglas, nails, pencils,
feather, and hair on lead sheet
46 1/2 x 46 1/2 in.
MMA Purchase, Clarence Y. Palitz, Jr. Gift and
various donors, 1987
1987.70
(cat. no. 7)

JOE ANDOE B. 1955

Untitled (Wreath), 1988
Oil on canvas
40 1/4 x 48 in.
MMA, Gift of Barbara and Eugene Schwartz, 1990
1990.341
(cat. no. 63)

Untitled (Horn), 1989
Oil on canvas
40 x 48 in.
MMA, Gift of Barbara and Eugene Schwartz, 1991
1991.320
(cat. no. 64)

JENNIFER BARTLETT B. 1941

One A.M., 1991–92
Oil on canvas
84 x 84 in.
MMA Purchase, Lila Acheson Wallace Gift, 1992
1992.341
(cat. no. 10)

ED BAYNARD B. 1940

An American Painting — For Rose Paul, 1979
Alkyd on canvas
48 3/4 x 60 1/4 in.
MMA, Gift of Barbara and Eugene Schwartz,
1980
1980.84
(cat. no. 23)

NELL BLAINE B. 1922

Big Table with Pomegranates, 1978
Oil on canvas
22 x 26 in.
MMA, Gift of Arthur W. Cohen, 1985
1985.36.1
(cat. no. 16)

WARREN BRANDT B. 1918

Beckmann Catalogue, 1986
Oil on canvas
40 1/4 x 54 1/2 in.
MMA, Gift of the Artist, 1991
1991.352
(cat. no. 25)

CARLYLE BROWN 1919–1964

Table with Figs and Lemons, 1952
Oil on canvas
27 1/2 x 36 1/2 in.
MMA, George A. Hearn Fund, 1952
52.162
(cat. no. 49)

AUDREY BULLER 1902–1984

Morning Glory, 1938
Oil on canvas
30 x 24 in.
MMA, George A. Hearn Fund, 1938
38.99
(cat. no. 3)

ROBERT CUMMING B. 1943

Burning Box, 1990
Oil on canvas
87 x 75 in.
MMA Purchase, Arthur Hoppock Hearn Fund, by
exchange, 1991
1991.104
(cat. no. 65)

STUART DAVIS 1892–1964

Studio Interior, 1917
Oil on canvas
18 7/8 x 23 in.
MMA, George A. Hearn Fund, 1994
1994. 412
(cat no. 26)

Edison Mazda, 1924
Oil on cardboard
24 1/2 x 18 5/8 in.
MMA Purchase, Mr. and Mrs. Clarence Y. Palitz,
Jr. Gift, in memory of her father, Nathan
Dobson, 1982
1982.10
(cat. no. 40)

RANDALL DEIHL B. 1946

Sweets, 1980
Oil on Masonite
35 1/2 x 45 in.
MMA Purchase, Frances and Benjamin
Benenson Foundation Inc. Gift, 1988
1988.52
(cat. no. 35)

PRESTON DICKINSON 1891–1930

Interior, 1924
Oil on canvas
31 x 28 in.
MMA, Gift of Edith C. Denniston, 1971
1971.126
(cat. no. 27)

JIM DINE B. 1935

The Heart, South of Naples, 1986
Oil on canvas
83 x 71 in.
MMA, Anonymous Gift, 1986
1986.404
(cat. no. 61)

RANDY DUDLEY B. 1950

Verifying Dissonant Statistics, 1981
Oil on canvas
21 5/8 x 27 5/8 in.
MMA, Arthur Hoppock Hearn Fund, 1983
1983.123.1
(cat. no. 36)

JEANNE DUVAL B. 1956

Still Life with Partridge and Corn, 1988
Oil on canvas
15 3/4 x 23 3/4 in.
MMA, Gift of Jane and Robert E. Carroll, 1991
1991.175.1
(cat. no. 18)

AARON FINK B. 1955

Untitled, 1987
Oil on canvas
30 x 24 in.
MMA, Arthur Hoppock Hearn Fund, 1989
1989.60
(cat. no. 62)

JANET FISH B. 1938

Raspberries and Goldfish, 1981
Oil on canvas
72 x 64 in.
MMA Purchase, The Cape Branch Foundation
and Lila Acheson Wallace Gifts, 1983
1983.171
(cat. no. 17)

AUDREY FLACK B. 1931

Macarena of Miracles, 1971
Oil on canvas
66 x 46 in.
MMA, Gift of Paul F. Walter, 1979
1979.556
(cat. no. 58)

CHUCK FORSMAN B. 1944

Fay's Kitchen, 1971
Oil on canvas
29 x 33 in.
MMA, Gift of Adam Baumgold, 1983
1983.583
(cat. no. 52)

JANE FREILICHER B. 1924

Bread and Bricks, 1984
Oil on canvas
24 x 30 in.
MMA, Gift of Dr. and Mrs. Robert E. Carroll, 1986
1986.159.2
(cat. no. 8)

The Lute Player, 1993
Oil on canvas
36 x 36 in.
MMA, Kathryn E. Hurd Fund, 1995
1995.133
(cat. no. 11)

A. E. GALLATIN 1881–1952

Number 28 (Still Life), 1940
Oil on canvas
24$^1/8$ x 20$^1/8$ in.
MMA, Gift of Jerry Leiber, 1985
1985.440.2
(cat. no. 45)

LEE GATCH 1902–1968

The Thorn, 1953
Oil on canvas
31$^1/2$ x 39$^1/2$ in.
MMA, The Edward Joseph Gallagher III Memorial Collection, Gift of Edward J. Gallagher Jr., 1954
54.10.1
(cat. no. 5)

GEORGE GROSZ 1893–1959

Still Life with Walnuts, 1937
Oil on canvas board
24 x 19$^7/8$ in.
MMA, George A. Hearn Fund, 1939
39.48.2
(cat. no. 14)

SAMUEL HALPERT 1884–1930

The Red Tablecloth, 1915
Oil on canvas
40 x 30 in.
MMA, Anonymous Loan
1994.394
(cat. no. 39)

MARSDEN HARTLEY 1877–1943

White Flower, ca. 1917
Oil on wood
16 x 12 in.
MMA, Gift of Rebecca and Raphael Soyer, 1983
1983.538
(cat. no. 19)

The Virgin of Guadalupe, 1919
Oil on cardboard
31 x 23$^7/8$ in.
MMA, Alfred Stieglitz Collection, 1949
49.70.44
(cat. no. 56)

Banquet of Silence, 1935–36
Oil on canvas board
19$^7/8$ x 15$^7/8$ in.
MMA, Alfred Stieglitz Collection, 1949
49.92.1
(cat. no. 12)

JOSEPH HIRSCH 1910–1981

Melons, 1962
Oil on canvas
13 $^3/16$ x 16$^1/4$ in.
MMA, Gift of Rita and Daniel Fraad, 1978
1978.509.7
(cat. no. 50)

E. McKNIGHT KAUFFER 1891–1954

Sunflowers, 1921
Oil on canvas
36 x 24 in.
MMA Purchase, The Mrs. Claus von Bulow Fund Gift, 1987
1987.5
(cat. no. 20)

FRANZ KLINE 1910–1962

Still Life with Puppet, ca. 1940
Oil on canvas
16$^1/4$ x 14$^1/4$ in.
MMA, Gift of Theodore J. Edlich, Jr., 1987
1987.463.3
(cat. no 46)

KARL KNATHS 1891–1971

Basket Bouquet, 1950
Oil on canvas
36 x 48 in.
MMA, Gift of Charles and Helen L. Friedman, 1964
64.144
(cat. no. 22)

JOHN KOCH 1909–1978

The Antiquarian, 1954
Oil on Masonite
16⁹/₁₆ x 12¹/₁₆ in.
MMA, Arthur Hoppock Hearn Fund, 1954
54.112
(cat. no. 30)

WALT KUHN 1887–1949

Apples from Dorset, Vermont, 1937
Oil on canvas
25 x 30 in.
MMA, Gift of Douglas Dillon, 1980
1980.238
(cat. no. 13)

YASUO KUNIYOSHI 1889–1953

Broken Objects, 1944
Oil on canvas
30 x 50¹/₄ in.
MMA, Gift of Mr. and Mrs. Allan D. Emil, 1963
63.189
(cat. no. 47)

LUIGI LUCIONI 1900–1988

Pears with Pewter, 1930
Oil on canvas
20¹/₄ x 28¹/₈ in.
MMA, George A. Hearn Fund, 1934
34.63
(cat. no. 41)

LOREN MacIVER B. 1909

Hardware (Quincaillerie), 1954
Oil on canvas
36 x 28 in.
MMA Purchase, Maria-Gaetana Matisse Gift, 1993
1993.278
(cat. no. 31)

Hearth, 1957
Oil on plaster on Masonite
49⁵/₈ x 34⁵/₈ in.
MMA Purchase, Marie-Gaetana Matisse Gift, 1993
1993.280
(cat. no. 32)

HENRY LEE McFEE 1886–1953

Still Life with Striped Curtain, 1931
Oil on canvas
30¹/₄ x 40 in.
MMA, George A. Hearn Fund, 1933
33.105
(cat. no. 42)

MAUD CABOT MORGAN B. 1903

September Still Life, 1938
Oil on canvas board
20 x 24 in.
MMA, George A. Hearn Fund, 1938
38.177
(cat. no. 15)

WALTER MURCH 1907–1967

Isotope, 1950
Oil on canvas
19³/₄ x 19¹/₄ in.
MMA, George A. Hearn Fund, 1952
52.180
(cat. no. 48)

CATHERINE MURPHY B. 1946

Blue Blanket, 1990
Oil on canvas
52³/₄ x 66 in.
MMA Purchase, Arthur Hoppock Hearn Fund, by exchange, 1991
1991.103
(cat. no. 9)

DONA NELSON B. 1952

Daily News, 1983
Oil on canvas
84 x 60 in.
MMA Purchase, Emma P. Ziprik Memorial Fund Gift, in memory of Fred and Emma P. Ziprik, 1984
1984.266
(cat. no. 37)

GEORGIA O'KEEFFE 1887–1986

Corn, Dark I, 1924
Oil on composition board
31 3/4 x 11 7/8 in.
MMA, Alfred Stieglitz Collection, 1950
50.236.1
(cat. no. 1)

Clam Shell, 1930
Oil on canvas
24 x 36 in.
MMA, Alfred Stieglitz Collection, 1962
62.258
(cat. no. 57)

SABINA OTT B. 1955

Book of Hours: Winter, 1985
Oil on canvas
54 x 48 in.
MMA, Edith C. Blum Fund, 1985
1985.257a,b
(cat. no. 38)

HORACE PIPPIN 1888–1946

Victorian Parlor, II, 1945
Oil on canvas
25 1/4 x 30 in.
MMA, Arthur Hoppock Hearn Fund, 1958
58.26
(cat. no. 28)

REGINALD POLLACK B. 1924

Interior, 1958
Oil on canvas
28 3/4 x 36 3/4 in.
MMA, Anonymous Gift, 1993
1993.432
(cat. no. 33)

FAIRFIELD PORTER 1907–1975

Lizzie at the Table, 1958
Oil on canvas
36 1/2 x 45 1/2 in.
MMA, Bequest of Arthur M. Bullowa, 1993
1993.406.2
(cat. no. 34)

PRISCILLA WARREN ROBERTS B. 1916

Carpet Bag Days, 1952
Oil on Masonite
30 x 13 5/8 in.
MMA, Arthur Hoppock Hearn Fund, 1953
53.17
(cat. no. 29)

JAMES ROSENQUIST B. 1933

Gift Wrapped Doll #16, 1992
Oil on canvas
60 x 60 in.
MMA Purchase, Lila Acheson Wallace Gift, 1993
1993.340.1
(cat. no. 66)

RAYMOND SAUNDERS B. 1934

Something About Something, 1963
Oil and charcoal on canvas
65 1/8 x 38 in.
MMA Purchase, Hugo Kastor Fund, by exchange, 1994
1994.366
(cat. no. 51)

DAVID SMITH 1906–1965

Seashell and Map, 1933
Oil on canvas
26 x 36 in.
MMA Purchase, Lila Acheson Wallace Gift, 1983
1983.438
(cat. no. 2)

RUFINO TAMAYO 1899–1991

The White Fruit Bowl, 1938
Oil on canvas
18 x 23 5/8 in.
MMA, From the Collection of Dr. and Mrs.
Samuel Ernest Sussman,
Bequest of Blanche Risa Sussman, 1990
1991.129.6
(cat. no. 44)
(Reproduction authorized by the Olga and
Rufino Tamayo Foundation, A.C.)

MARK TANSEY B. 1949

Still Life, 1982
Oil on canvas
62 x 46 in.
MMA Purchase, Louis and Bessie Adler
Foundation, Inc. Gift (Seymour M.
Klein, President), 1982
1982.359
(cat. no. 24)

BRADLEY WALKER TOMLIN 1899–1953

Burial, 1943
Oil on canvas
30 1/4 x 44 1/4 in.
MMA, George A. Hearn Fund, 1943
43.159.5
(cat. no. 4)

JAMES VALERIO B. 1938

Still Life with Decoy, 1983
Oil on canvas
84 x 100 in.
MMA Purchase, Lila Acheson Wallace Gift, 1985
1985.242
(cat. no. 54)

ANDY WARHOL 1930–1987

Still Life, 1976
Acrylic and silkscreen on canvas
72 x 86 in.
MMA, Gift of Richard and Peggy Danziger, 1986
1986.402
(cat. no. 59)

FRANKLIN WATKINS 1894–1972

White Roses, 1945
Oil on canvas
27 x 33$^1/_8$ in
MMA, George A. Hearn Fund, 1945
45.157.1
(cat. no. 21)

MAX WEBER 1881–1961

The Celadon Vase, ca. 1933
Oil on canvas
30 x 36 in.
MMA, George A. Hearn Fund, 1934
34.66
(cat. no. 43)

JONATHAN WEINBERG B. 1957

The Wheel, St. Catherine, 1983
Oil on canvas
60 x 40 in.
MMA, Edith C. Blum Fund, 1983
1983.585
(cat. no. 6)

AMY WEISKOPF B. 1957

Still Life with Clock, 1986
Oil on canvas
19$^5/_8$ x 27$^1/_2$ in.
MMA, Gift of Jane and Robert E. Carroll, 1991
1991. 175.8
(cat. no. 55)

JEROME WITKIN B. 1939

Number 4818, 1985
Oil on canvas
25 x 31 in.
MMA, Gift of Dr. and Mrs. Robert E. Carroll, 1987
1987.460.2
(cat. no. 60)

PAUL WONNER B. 1920

*"Dutch" Still Life with Orchids, Postcard View of
Paris, and "Death of Marat,"* 1983
Acrylic on canvas
70 x 50 in.
MMA, George A. Hearn Fund, 1983
1983.454
(cat. no. 53)

NATIONAL PATRONS

Mr. and Mrs. Philip Anschutz
Amy C. Arkin
Mr. and Mrs. Frank B. Bennett
Mr. and Mrs. Winslow W. Bennett
Nancy Benson
Mr. and Mrs. Robert A. Belfer
Mrs. Edwin A. Bergman
Mrs. George F. Berlinger
Mr. and Mrs. Leonard Block
Mr. and Mrs. Donald J. Blum
Mr. and Mrs. Duncan E. Boeckman
Melva Bucksbaum
Mr. and Mrs. Andrew L. Camden
Mr. and Mrs. George M. Cheston
Mrs. Paul A. Cohen
Elaine Terner Cooper
Marina Couloucoudis
Catherine G. Curran
Dr. and Mrs. David R. Davis
Sandra Deitch
Beth Rudin DeWoody
Mr. and Mrs. C. Douglas Dillon
Mr. and Mrs. Herbert Doan
Mrs. Lester Eisner
Mr. and Mrs. Oscar Feldman
Mr. and Mrs. James A. Fisher
Bart Friedman and Wendy Stein
Barbara Goldsmith
Marion E. Greene
Mr. and Mrs. Gerald Grinstein
Leo S. Guthman

Mr. and Mrs. Frederic C. Hamilton
Mrs. Wellington S. Henderson
Elaine P. Kend
Mr. and Mrs. Robert P. Kogod
Mr. and Mrs. Anthony M. Lamport
Natalie Ann Lansburgh
Katherine Lawrence
Mrs. Robert H. Levi
Mrs. Richard Livingston
Mr. and Mrs. Jeffrey M. Loewy
Mr. and Mrs. Lester B. Loo
Mr. and Mrs. Mark O.L. Lynton
Richard Manoogian
Mr. and Mrs. Melvin Mark, Jr.
Mr. and Mrs. Alan M. May
Mrs. Eugene McDermott
Mr. and Mrs. Robert Menschel
Mr. and Mrs. Eugene Mercy, Jr.
Mrs. Peter Roussel Norman
George P. O'Leary
James H. Ottaway, Jr.
Patricia M. Patterson
Mr. and Mrs. Mark Perlbinder
Mr. and Mrs. Nicholas R. Petry
Mr. and Mrs. Charles I. Petschek
Mr. and Mrs. John W. Pitts
Mr. and Mrs. Lawrence Pollock, Jr.
Howard Rachofsky
Edward R. Roberts
Mr. and Mrs. Jonathan P. Rosen
Mr. and Mrs. Robert J. Rosenberg
Walter S. Rosenberry, III
Mr. and Mrs. Milton F. Rosenthal
Mr. and Mrs. Richard Rosenthal
Felice T. Ross
Mr. and Mrs. Lawrence Ruben
Mr. and Mrs. Douglas R. Scheumann
Marcia Schloss
Mr. and Mrs. Paul C. Schorr, III
Mr. and Mrs. Alan Schwartz
Mr. and Mrs. Joseph Seviroli
Mr. and Mrs. George A. Shutt
Elaine Siegel
Mr. and Mrs. Gilbert Silverman

Mr. and Mrs. Robert Sosnick
Mr. and Mrs. James G. Stevens
Mr. and Mrs. Harry F. Stimpson, Jr.
Rosalie Taubman
Mrs. Norman Tishman
Mr. and Mrs. William B. Troy
Dianne Wallace and Lowell M. Schulman
Chryssa Vardea
Mr. and Mrs. Robert C. Warren
Mr. and Mrs. Alan Weeden
Mr. and Mrs. Guy A. Weill
Mr. and Mrs. David Welles
Mr. and Mrs. T. Evans Wyckoff

BENEFACTORS CIRCLE

Arthur G. Altshul
Mr. and Mrs. Steven Ames
Mr. and Mrs. Howard R. Berlin
Mrs. Brooke Blake
Ruth Bowman
Mr. and Mrs. B. Gerald Cantor
Constance R. Caplan
Mr. and Mrs. Donald M. Cox
David L. Davies and John D. Weeden
Mr. and Mrs. Kenneth N. Dayton
Madeleine Feher
Mr. and Mrs. Miles Fiterman
Mr. and Mrs. John A. Friede
Dr. Arthur Gillman
Mrs. Melville W. Hall
Mr. and Mrs. Lee Hills
Mr. and Mrs. Theodore Hochstim
Harry Kahn
Mr. and Mrs. Peter Kimmelman
Mr. and Mrs. Gilbert H. Kinney
Mr. and Mrs. Richard S. Lane
Mr. and Mrs. Robert E. Linton
Mr. and Mrs. Henry Luce III
Jeanne Lang Mathews
Mr. and Mrs. Frederick R. Mayer
Mr. and Mrs. C. Blake McDowell, Jr.
Mr. and Mrs. Robert M. Meltzer
Barbara Babcock Millhouse
Mr. and Mrs. Roy R. Neuberger
Sunny Norton
Mr. and Mrs. Leon B. Polsky
Mr. and Mrs. Rudi H. Scheidt
Mr. and Mrs. Rudolph B. Schulhof
Mr. and Mrs. Jan I. Shrem
Barbara Slifka
Ann C. Stephens
Mr. and Mrs. John W. Straus
Mr. and Mrs. David J. Supino
Mr. and Mrs. Jeff Tarr
Mrs. George W. Ullman
Mr. and Mrs. Irwin Weinberg
Mr. and Mrs. Martin S. Weinberg
Mrs. Keith S. Wellin
Mr. and Mrs. Dave H. Williams